Art and Design in Modern

Custom
Fixed-Blade
Knives

Art and Design in Modern

Custom Fixed-Blade Knives

Dr. David Darom

Series producer
Paolo Saviolo

Biography Editor
Bud Lang

Photography
Eric Eggly - PointSeven Inc., USA
Francesco Pachì, ITALY
Jim Cooper - SharpByCoop.com, USA
Dr. Fred Carter, Mitchell Lum, Steve Towell,
Tom Lansing, Dino Petrocelli, Scott Slobodian,
Jim Kelso, KnifeArt.com, Louise Bilodeau,
Larry Linkous, Michel Gauvint, Rob Nicoll,
Marc Mesplié, Alain Miville-Deschenes,
Tom Kishida, Leon (Lonnie) Kapp, Jessica Marcotte
and Paolo Saviolo

CHARTWELL
BOOKS, INC.

All texts were written by the artists and edited by
Dr. David Darom

Photography:
The photographers whose work is depicted throughout this book hold the
copyrights to the images they created. They authorized the author to digitally
manipulate the original backgrounds, creating new ones for the book.

Digital image processing: Dr. David Darom and Nir Darom

Book Design: Nomi Morag, Jerusalem, Israel
Copyeditor: Evelyn Katrak, Jerusalem, Israel
Proof reading: Dr. Tuvia Zisner, Ra'anana, Israel
Color conversions and color enhancing: Ya'acov Laloum, Jerusalem, Israel
Printers, Macintosh computers and proofing materials: Pal-ron Ltd.,
Jerusalem, Israel. palron-j@palron.co.il
Scanning images: Panorama Ltd., Jerusalem, Israel. info@panorama.co.il

Each knifemaker is granted the use of parts or all of the material in their
section for their own needs, providing this book is quoted as their source.

© 2007 White Star s.p.a.
Via Candido Sassone, 22/24
13100 Vercelli, Italy
www.whitestar.it

This edition published in 2007 by
CHARTWELL BOOKS, INC.
A division of BOOK SALES, INC.
114 Northfield Avenue
Edison, New Jersey 08837
USA

ISBN-13: 978-0-7858-2268-4
ISBN-10: 0-7858-2268-2

REPRINTS:
1 2 3 4 5 6   11 10 09 08 07

Printed in China

Title page:
"Arwen" and "Angelic" by Ron Appleton, 2004
"Arwen", the three-position push-dagger, and its fixed-blade sister, **"Angelic"**,
were created from the same titanium billet. Both have a similar steel blade
geometry and a matching color scheme in the anodized Ti handle.
Ron kept the lines of the fixed-blade open, flowing and simple while trying to
incorporate in its shape some of the curved nature of his folder, "Arwen", adding
an original open-floral-design guard. Overall lengths are 8 5/8" (220 mm) for the
folder and 10 11/16" (272 mm) for "Angelic".

Table of Contents

Preface

In March 2003, at the East Coast Custom Knife Show in New York, my book on custom folding knives was introduced to the public by Paolo Saviolo and myself. It was a new concept, a vision come true, and it was born through the exciting collaboration of many during an intensive 18 months. A labor of love that bore beautiful fruit.

But there and then, in the elegant setting of the New York Knife Show, I was confronted with a problem. Several of the world's leading custom knifemakers, echoing each others' thoughts and those of many other knifemakers and collectors worldwide, politely suggested that only half the job was done... They challenged me to complete what I had already begun, in a second book of similar design, this time showing the art of modern custom fixed-blade knives.

This sent me back more than 35 years, when stories about Bo Randall and his legendary custom fixed-blade knives were circulating around the world, setting me on an exciting journey into the world of modern steel blades. Over these decades, I have watched with great fascination the changes that visually transformed the art of hand-made knives into what it is today - from virtually indestructible and beautifully made highly functional hand-forged knives into a craftsmanship and artistry that created original, never-to-be-actually-used objects of art. Here, the sky was the limit, allowing talented artists to show the world their creations, putting together one-of-a kind art knives with their newly acquired art of working with steel and combining it with extraordinary embellishments. The field was open to craftspeople from many disciplines: sculptors, jewelers, etc. In studios around the world, these talented men and women combined their newly born passion with wondrous vitality and artistic capability to create art knives. They began using modern-age techniques and a variety of high-tech materials in their art, combining these with traditional styles and materials. Forging together various metallic elements, they proceeded to come up with exciting Damascus steel and intricate Mosaic Damascus patterns in steel. This became an art in itself, reaching near ultimate levels of perfection and accuracy using modern metallurgic techniques. Then came Timascus, a very light and durable "Damascus" created by forging different grades of Titanium, rather than steel, which can be heat-blued to a spectacular array of colors.

Collectors were intrigued and easily captivated by the fascination of this modern custom knife art, and beautifully finished hand-forged cutlery became in great demand all over the world. Regretfully, these one-of-a-kind hand-made art pieces are often shipped directly to collectors, only to be kept "hidden" away in their private collections and never exposed to the general public. In this book on custom fixed-blade knives and in my previous volume on custom folding knives, I have tried to create a printed "Hall of Fame" to exhibit this contemporary art, bringing forth its beauty for all art lovers to enjoy, wherever they are.

Choosing from among a long list of very talented custom fixed-blade makers, all of whom deserved to be represented in this new book, proved again to be a difficult task. It kept me awake for many, many nights, before I began to approach the artists. Several considerations guided the selection in making a list of fixed-blade artists who would eventually go down in history as representatives of this art at the beginning of the third millennium.

In making the final decisions I considered, in addition to my own personal aesthetic preferences, visual originality, stylistic diversity and my desire to mingle young, promising artists with world-renowned veterans. Quality of design and workmanship, steels used, beauty of the embellishments and the visual appeal of the final pieces all combined here to give the world a representative insight into this wondrous art. I finally chose the 26 makers to be featured artists and devoted eight pages each to the presentation of their art. More than 30 additional custom fixed-blade makers are also represented in the

Opposite, clockwise from top right:
1 With my son Nir Darom, discussing finishihg touches to the illustrations for the book.
2 With Featured Artists at the 2003 Milan Knife Show. From the left: Dietmar Kressler, Zaza Revishvili. Dr. David Darom, Francesco Pachi, Charlie Bennica, Conny Persson, Roger Bergh and Scott Slobodian
3 At the San Diego Art Knife Invitational Show (November 2003). Standing, from the left: Phil Lobred, Dr. Fred Carter, Buster Warenski, Julie Warenski, Van Barnett, Dellana, Steve Hoel, John W. Smith, Jurgen Steinau, Tim Hancock, Steve Schwarzer, Kaj Embretsen, C. Gray Taylor, Dwight L. Towell, Dr. David Darom, Steve R. Johnson, Henry H. Frank, Nicole Reverdy, Ron Appleton, Mrs. Yoshihara, Wolfgang Loerchner, Ray Appleton and Larry Fuegen
Sitting, from the left: Michael Walker, Tim Herman, Bob Loveless., Dietmar F. Kressler, T.M. Dowel, Yoshindo Yoshihara and Pierre Reverdy
4 With Don Cowles at the 2004 Blade Show.
5 At the 2004 Blade Show in Atlanta: (from the left) Dennis Greenbaum, Dr. David Darom, Ron Nott and Robert Eggerling, after four days of fine-tuning the concept details for a surprise third book on custom knife-making

book, the beauty of their knives displayed in the introduction and on one-page illustrations throughout the book.

Here again, all the knives have been portrayed on non-distracting backgrounds - with the consent of the world class photographers whose photos, taken over a period of several years, were digitally manipulated. This demanded from me over 1,000 hours of computer work, carefully removing images from their original backgrounds, including several knives in a single illustration and enlarging various sections of the knives to show, in detail, what this art is all about. The "manipulated" backgrounds were created to complement the beauty of the knives, and a different hue was chosen to maintain reader interest throughout each artist's 8-page section.

These 8-page sections, dedicated to each of the 26 Featured Artists (arranged alphabetically after the introduction), consist of the following:
- The artist's picture, biography and (signed) personal statement
- A photographic sequence showing the artist creating certain specific features of a fixed-blade knife made specially for the book
- A full-page illustration of the completed "Featured Knife" created for the book
- Five pages showing choice custom knives made by the artist in recent years, through November 2004

I decided to open the book with full-page illustrations of fixed-blade knives made by two of the most promising young custom knifemakers in the world today. The title page shows a matching pair of knives made for the book by **Ron Appleton**, one of them being the first modern fixed-blade knife made by him. Page 6 shows the breathtaking creation by **André Andersson** of Sweden, a rising superstar in the world of hand-made art knives, also made specially for the book.

My deepest thanks go to all the wonderful people who shared this adventure with me, many of them for the second time, and especially:

To **Phil Lobred** who, by inviting me to the 2001 and 2003 AKI shows in San Diego, enabled me to present my

Opposite:
The "Tools"
All the final versions of the pictures for the book were created on a G4 Macintosh computer, using Adobe Photoshop 8.0 CS software and the fantastic 23" Apple Cinema HD Display. Most of the photographs were originally shot with various high-end digital cameras while the rest were scanned into the computer from film. During the process of digitally manipulating the images, great care was taken not to interfere with the actual art work. The knives are therefore reproduced as close to their true colors as was possible. Only the backgrounds were changed, deleting the original ones and creating new ones in various plain colors, choosing different hues for each artist. Constant feedback from the artists allowed me to accurately reproduce the shades and colors of over 350 photographs shown throughout the book, depicting more than 400 different knives and a variety of knifemaking processes. About 1,000 hours of computer work went into creating the final illustrations, carefully pulling images from their original backgrounds, including several knives in one picture and enlarging various sections to show, in detail, what this art is all about.

original concept for a book to the most prominent knife artists in the world, giving the first breath of life to the fulfillment of a dream.

To **Bud Lang**, editor, writer and publisher, who not only worked his magic on many texts throughout the book but also encouraged me along the way, becoming, over the past 5 years, a real friend. To **Dennis Greenbaum**, who knew how to trigger original ideas that later grew and evolved into exciting items throughout the book. To **Don Guild**, a collector of art knives, a man of great experience and a true friend, for his constant encouragement, his down-to-earth advice and for always being there for me with his continuous moral support. To **Leon (Lonnie) Kapp**, who introduced me to the Japanese sword and shares his vast knowledge with all of us throughout the pages of this book. To **Bob Glassman** and **Niel Ostroff**, who kept me up-to-date about everything concerning custom knifemakers.

To **Eric Eggly** of PointSeven Studios, **Francesco Pachì** and **Jim Cooper** of SharpByCoop.com, whose extraordinary

photography, together with that of **Dr. Fred Carter, Mitchell Lum**, Steve Towell, Tom Lansing, Dino Petrocelli, Scott Slobodian, Jim Kelso, KnifeArt.com, Louise Bilodeau, Larry Linkous, Michel Gauvint, Rob Nicoll, Marc Mesplié, Alain Miville-Deschenes, Tom Kishida, Leon (Lonnie) Kapp, Jessica Marcotte and **Paolo Saviolo** enabled me to produce this art book on modern hand-made fixed-blade knives. To Dave Cowles for his caricature of me for the copyright page.

To **Dr. Pierluigi Peroni** (Italy), a friend who was there for me when most needed, for his great contribution to the book and to the world of custom fixed-blade knives.

To **Dr. Larry Marton** (USA) and **Dr. Thad Kawakami-Wong** (Hawaii) for opening their private collections for photography, sharing with me their vast knowledge on art knives and knifemakers.

To my friend and world-class book designer **Mrs. Nomi Morag** who knew exactly how to fit every one of my ideas into a beautifully designed art book.

To Dr. **Tuvia Zisner** (Israel) who did an excellent job proof-reading all the texts in the book even though he was put under the great pressure of a very short, last minute, time limit.

Special thanks go to **Paolo Saviolo** of the Saviolo Publishing House, who believed in my vision, encouraged and backed me all the way, and took upon himself, with his unique Italian charm, the difficult job of distributing both my books all over the world.

Special thanks go also to each and every one of the artists whose exquisite creations made this book a "Hall of Fame" for the art of modern custom fixed-blade knives.

Last but not least, to my wife **Tehiya**, who is, among many other wonderful things, also my best critic, and to my children and grandchildren, who again had to put up with my long "disappearing acts" in front of the computer, this time for just over 16 months, while I totally plunged myself into other worlds. To **Nir**, my son, and **Naomi**, his wife, designers "par excellence", who checked and re-checked everything I did, improving every page in the book from cover to cover and bringing it to the final quality all of us can now be so proud of.

ﭏﭏﭏ ﭏﭏ

Dr. David Darom
March, 2005

Opposite, from the top:
Collecting custom knives
Serious collectors like to specialize, and in time, their taste matures and they get to recognize the knife designs that move and excite them most. A similar design-concept of a knife, made by various makers, each with his own style and personal touch, appeals to many collectors. When approaching the maker they will describe their preferred design to him. The maker then creates a knife, doing his artistic interpretation of their request along those guidelines. Shown here are knives of similar design-concept, made to order for the collector by some of the top early modern day custom knifemakers in the world: R.W. Loveless, S.R. Johnson, T.M. Dowell, and Gil Hibben. Full tang, drop-point hunters with ivory handles, scroll engraving and 3 ½ to 4 inch blades, dating from the early 80s to mid 90s. Hibben and Loveless were making custom knives in the 50s, Dowell and Johnson by the late 60s.
From the collection of Phil Lobred, USA

Modern Custom Knifemaking

By Dennis Greenbaum

It is 1:30 a.m. on a Thursday night, and a middle-aged Pennsylvania businessman and part-time knifemaker is trying to finish up a small boot knife he's been working on since the beginning of the week. He has been making knives for only just over a year, and his inexperience still shows every now and then, just as it has this particular evening. Hoping to have the new knife finished in time for the coming weekend's big knife show, he's run into a problem and it is too late to call anyone for advice.

Unfazed, he sets the knife down on the bench in his makeshift workshop, located in the family garage, and walks into the house. He sits down at the computer, logs onto the Internet and within minutes is connected to the world.

"Can anyone tell me what is the best angle to use for dovetailed bolsters, and is there an easy way to achieve the proper fit?" he types. Confident that he'll soon have a response, he gets up and walks down the hall to the kitchen to fix another cup of coffee, and by the time he returns, he has three answers to his query.

Across the ocean, in a small European town, it is just passed 7:30 a.m., and a leading German knifemaker is checking the on-line forums to see if there is anything interesting. He sees the question posed by the inexperienced American knifemaker, and of course knowing the appropriate answer, he quickly responds in detail.

Over the next 10 minutes, a similar response is posted by a maker in Australia, and yet another in Hawaii.

These four knifemakers, who share a common passion, are taking part in a revolution... one that, in a few short years, has forever changed the course of modern custom knifemaking.

W. D. "Bo" Randall (1909-1989)

USA

Bo Randall was born in Cincinnati, Ohio, in 1909, and in 1916 moved to Orlando with his family. In 1936, while at his summer home in Michigan, he saw a man scraping the bottom of a boat with a very fine hand-made knife. The knife did not dull under steady use and Bo, intrigued by the tool, learned that it had been made by William Scagle, the grandfather of modern hand-forged knives, and that it was definitely not for sale. Bo came back to Orlando and determined to make one just as good. So, with a leaf spring from an old car and whatever tools he could find plus about 20 hours of hard work, he turned out the first Randall Knife. On a hunting trip not long after, a hunting partner admired it so much that Bo gave it to him. This happened repeatedly for the next four or five hunting trips, until he began to see the demand for a really well-made knife by hunters and sportsman, and that started him off on what was to be his principal work for the rest of his life. His knives have become the best-known and most noted hand-made knives in the world. They have been mentioned both in novels and in histories and have been used extensively by hunters, soldiers and Marines, flyers and sailors, generals and infantrymen not to mention astronauts, government agents, celebrities, statesmen and royalty, and they are prized by collectors.

Bo Randall knives

from the collection of Guido Bitossi, Italy
Opposite, clockwise from the left:

Fourth RKSA (Randall Knives Society of America) Club Knife. 8" (203 mm) tool steel blade, double brass hilt, red, white and blue spacers, stag handle, duralluminium butt cup. Made in 2001.

Model #12, Little Bear Fighter with elephant ivory handle. 6" (152 mm) stainless steel blade, nickel-silver double hilt, smooth nickel-silver collar, natural elephant ivory tip with beautiful checks in the handle. Late 90s.

Model #25, "The Trapper". 5" (127 mm) blade of 1/4" stock, leather and stag handle. Drop-point Hunter similar to Model #11, but handle construction is reminiscent of 1930s design. One of the Randall best sellers. The first Randall knife in Guido Bitossi's collection.

Model #23, Fighter Unusual. This Model #23 "Gamemaster" should be named the "Fightmaster", as it is set up as a fighter with the nickel-silver # 1 style, double hilt. The maroon and blue micarta handle, no longer available from the Randall Shop, is finished out in a very nice, colorful handle showing concentric swirls. The 4 1/2" (114 mm) blade is 1/4" stainless stock. Late 90s.

Model Denmark Special non-catalog knife. 4 1/2" (114 mm) stainless steel blade, stag handle. Very rare because of the thickness of the blade. Mid 80s.

Model "Old Nordic Special". Randall Model Nordic Special, discontinued dealer special for Nordic Knives, 3 1/2" (89 mm) drop-point blade and thumb grip on the back. Single-hilt brass guard with brass and black spacers. Walnut handle with brass butt plate. Mid 80's.

Model #2 Stiletto. 4" (102 mm) stainless steel blade, brass double-hilt, brass and black spacers, concave walnut handle, dome shaped brass butt cap. This is one of the Non-Catalog Models II. Mid-late 90s.

There is perhaps no other object that can be so universally found in households the world over, as a knife. Most homes have at least several knives, perhaps even dozens. They are used in the kitchen, at the dining room table, at the work bench, in the sewing box, for outdoor sport, and for everyday carrying. With so many different uses, the variety can be nothing less than amazing. In the majority of these households, the members take the knives for granted, never once thinking about the origins of any one particular knife. Especially in a day and age when most knives are mass-produced and made well enough to be at least serviceable, there's not much reason to give that knife they're using more than a passing thought.

Although time and invention have changed the world, the basic utilitarian aspects of a knife have largely remained unchanged throughout the centuries. But with the advent of modern technology, methods for making those knives have, in many ways, gone through significant changes - what with robotic production, digital accuracy, and state-of-the-art blade and handle materials.

Through it all there's been the lone custom knifemaker. Over the centuries, the knowledge required for making a knife was mostly passed down from generation to generation. Or perhaps, if he had the desire, a young lad might be lucky enough to be taken on as a maker's apprentice. In more recent decades, those interested could perhaps seek out an accomplished knifemaker and with luck, be allotted enough time in his presence to learn a thing or two.

However the knowledge was acquired, ultimately it still came down to the knifemaker, working alone in pursuit of a passion, and all the while doing his best to acquire the skills necessary to raise his own personal bar. This was a painfully slow process of learning. So much of it was trial and error. Like most any other craft, those who did learn its secrets kept them closely guarded. A father passed them along to his son or a master knifemaker took on a sole apprentice. Methods were kept close to the fold... if they were kept at all. As a result, all too often when a maker passed away the secrets passed with him.

Enter the modern age. And along with it, 20th-century forms of audio and visual communication: telephone, radio, TV, and modern periodicals like newspapers and magazines. With time, distance and geography no longer an issue, stories about skilled craftsmen and pictures of their work could now quickly be spread to all four corners of the earth. With the latest edition of a monthly knife magazine laid out before him, a knifemaker in Texas could see the image of a knife only recently made by a fellow maker located thousands of miles away, perhaps in Canada, or France. Looking at a photograph he might exclaim to himself, "Gee, I like the way he carved that ivory handle!" And armed with that fresh bit of inspiration, he might perhaps attempt a similar technique on his newest knife. Different styles of knives, incorporating different techniques for making and embellishing, were now being shown the world over, often popularized by a story or a photo.

It was all well and good that a knifemaker could observe from a photograph what another was doing on the other side of the globe. However, with the exception of the occasional "how-to" articles in one or two knife publications, he was still (mostly) limited to his own skill and ingenuity, and good old-fashioned trial and error. With a desire to share their passion with others, a handful of experienced knifemakers started up clubs and organizations devoted to promoting the making of knives. Unlike other artisans and craftsmen the world over, who steadfastly maintain the tradition of keeping their secrets closely guarded, these expert "bladesmiths" were happy to educate others; as long as someone showed an interest, most makers were more than willing to teach. Through their efforts, and with the help of their rather unique attitude of sharing both knowledge and technique, a new generation of makers appeared, albeit still somewhat limited in number. As long as "students" needed to be instructed one-on-one, there were still only so many that could be trained or even exposed to the principles and basics of custom knifemaking.

In the 1990s the world changed the way it communicated, and custom knifemaking changed along with it.

Bill Moran
USA

Born in 1925 in Maryland, USA, Bill Moran is one of the founders of the American Bladesmithing Society. He makes his knives by hand - from the forging of the steel, to the precious metal inlay and carving on the handle, to the stitching of the sheath. He has been doing this for over 60 years, and has become known as one of the world's leading bladesmiths. Moran's knives are well balanced, and even his Bowie knives feel light and have blades that are sharp enough to shave with or, just as easily cut timber.

"Southwestern Bowie"

A very fine example of Bill Moran's Southwestern Bowie with a Curly Maple grip and Bill's silver-wire-inlay "signature". The handle on this knife is somewhat atypical of a Moran Bowie, making it a rare collector's piece. The knife comes with a snake-raised leather scabbard, wood-lined, and with a steel throat.

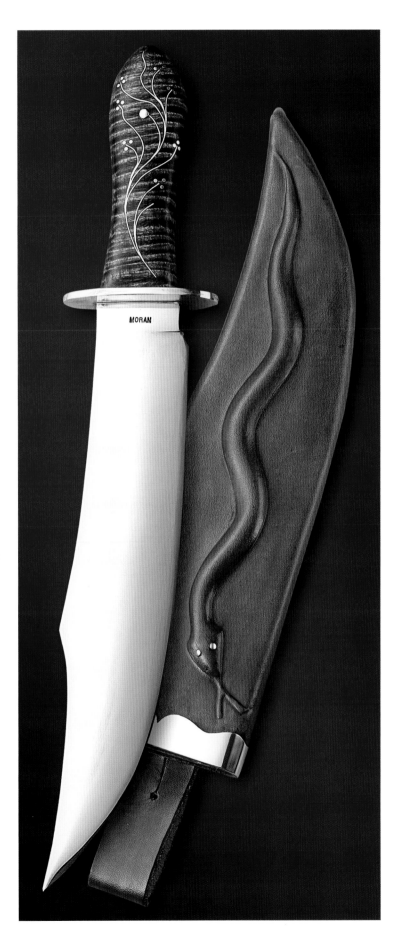

Opposite, on the left:

James A. Schmidt

USA

Jim Schmidt was born in Schenectady, New York in 1940, made occasional knives as he grew up, and started knifemaking in earnest in 1974 while living in Charlton, New York. The master of sole authorship, Jim made highly sought after knives until his untimely demise on July 20, 2000.

"Viking Dagger", 1992

An artistic giant, Jim Schmidt was a gentle and thoughtful individual. Obtaining one of his masterpiece knives took patience and many years. Since his time was spoken for so far in advance, getting him to try something brand new was a challenge, but Jim agreed to make this dagger, and it took nearly 6 months to do so. The Ladder pattern Damascus blade, forged of 203 and W2 steels, is as close to perfection as humanly possible, the file work is remarkable and a magnificent small dagger is hidden in the fossil walrus ivory handle. When this knife was completed and displayed at a show, many orders for a similar piece were placed. Unfortunately, no other will ever exist. Overall length 15 3/4" (400 mm).

Opposite, on the right:

Ron Newton

USA

Ron Newton was born in Corpus Christi, Texas in 1960 and now resides in London, Arkansas as a fulltime bladesmith. Ron, an ABS Mastersmith, began full time knifemaking in 1996 and is the only individual ever to win every award given by that society.

"Gent's Bowie", 2002

A week before Rick Fields' passing, Dr. Larry Marton visited him and found a man, excited as ever about his life's passions for natural materials and scrimshaw. During their conversation, Rick identified 2 pieces of fossil walrus ivory that he was particularly anxious to have made into knives. The knife shown here is the first product of that interaction. Rick wanted Ron Newton to make the knife and Gary Williams (Garbo) to scrim it. On the reverse side of the handle of this memorial piece, Gary Williams scrimmed a small broken branch – a farewell to Rick. The Diamond Ladder pattern Damascus blade is forged of W2 and 15N20 steels. The guard and finial knob are nickel-silver. Vine-fileworked, gold anodized titanium liners. Overall length 12 1/4" (311 mm).

Both knives from the collection of Dr. Larry Marton, USA

Dusty Moulton

USA

Born in 1951, Dusty Moulton grew up in the Eastern Oregon Desert, fishing, hunting and working on local ranches. His knifemaking career began in 1991, self-taught from reading and watching tutorial videos. In 2002 he also learned to engrave his knives. He currently builds and engraves about 50 knives a year on a full-time basis.

From the left:

"Predator", 2003

The handle is made of African waterbuck antelope horn. Damascus is 1095 & nickel by Jim Ferguson.
Overall length 11 1/2" (287 mm).

"Sliver", 2004

The handle material is Paua shell and the Damascus is 1095 & nickel by Jim Ferguson.
Overall length 10 3/4" (273 mm).

"Talon", 2003

The handle is made of elephant ivory. Damascus is 1095 & nickel by Jim Ferguson.
Overall length 11 1/2" (287 mm).

The Internet quickly became the world's most powerful education tool. With the ability to access information and knowledge from nearly anywhere on the planet, people flocked to the Internet as their newest, and in many cases primary, source for education.

"Chat rooms" started up places on-line where like-minded individuals could go at any time of the day or night and share their common interest. These were followed by more formally structured on-line environments, called "forums". We now have a number of well-populated knife-related forums with memberships totaling in the tens of thousands! Log onto any of these forums and one can always find someone talking about knives. While "production" knives are discussed side-by-side along with "custom" knives, there's no denying that all participants share a common interest: how are knives made, who's making them, what was used to make the knife, and how can they make a knife?

With all this information so readily available, people from all walks of life are getting interested in knifemaking. These days you're just as likely to find a New York accountant finishing a wonderfully embellished pocketknife in his basement workshop, as you are a former Canadian school teacher, looking for something to do in his retirement, discovering a latent ability to turn out exquisite, little, fixed blades knives. Many are drawn into the craft by a life-long fascination with knives, never before occurring to them that they might actually be able to make one on their own. Others fall into it almost by accident, a chance peek into any one of the online knife forums, and the next thing you know they're hooked.

However it happens, if someone wants to learn about knifemaking, or just further existing skills, it's all there for the taking. Hundreds, if not thousands of custom knifemakers the world over, more than happy to share their passion with others, are online all hours of the day or night, exchanging techniques, useful tips, "how to" tutorials, and photos of their latest creations. And the knives just keep getting better and better as the old methods meet up with the new, and the information age reaches out to a whole world full of potential custom knifemakers.

Above, from the top:

Todd Begg

USA

Born in Seattle, Washington, USA in 1971, Todd Begg has been making knives since 1997. Working with a variety of high-tech modern alloys, he developed his own style of Integral fixed-blades with what he calls his "In-Line" handle treatment, producing bold and dramatic designs. Todd turned full time knifemaker in 2003.

Mach-1

Integral made of S30V steel with a green canvas micarta handle.

Overall length 7" (175 mm).

The Emlum

Integral made of S30V steel with a stabilized Amboyna burl handle.

Overall length 7" (175 mm).

The Skarmaker

Integral made of S30V steel with a Damascus steel handle.

Overall length 7" (175 mm).

Opposite, from the left:

Jan Slezak,

Czech Republic

Born in the Czechoslovakia in 1964, Jan made and sold his first knife at the age of 25. In 1990 he became a full-time knifemaker. In 1993 he developed his unique style of sculpturing and pierce-carving his knives.

"Koala", 2001

Taking about 400 hours to finish, this Integral is made of Czech steel (170042) and 24k gold. The knife has won several awards at international knife shows.

Overall length 8 9/16" (220 mm).

"Silent Hunter", 2000

An Integral carved out of a solid bar of ATS-34, using 24k gold for the eyes. This knife has won several international awards, including the 2003 W. W. Cronk Award. 400 hours to complete.

Overall length 8 1/4" (210 mm).

"Hummingbirds", 2001

Carved ATS-34 and buffalo horn.

Overall length 8 9/16" (220 mm).

Along with all the new custom makers, comes a whole new breed of knife buyers and knife collectors. They are well informed, and they have the knifeworld at their fingertips as they cruise through the Internet reading about the latest and greatest in the world of custom knives. Never before have so many been able to so quickly view a new knife, fresh from the maker's bench. Most modern knifemakers, ever aware of the potential of the Internet, have taught themselves how to photograph their knives, and get them quickly posted online for all the world to see. Every day, more and more people are being exposed to a world they never even knew existed. Far larger than most people may have thought, the world of custom knifemaking is coming into its own, and beginning to achieve the recognition it so richly deserves.

It's a revolution, and it's spreading. And the world of modern custom knifemaking has been forever changed, for the better.

Opposite, from the left:

Dellana
USA

A Featured Artist in volume-1 on custom folding knives, Dellana, born in 1955, in the USA, occasionally makes sole authorship fixed-blade art knives, exhibiting her great skills as a jeweler and knifemaker.

"The King's Companion", 1998
Dagger, with a 324 layer 203E & W-2 steel Damascus blade. Bolsters of nickel Damascus. 14k yellow gold, garnets and premium Mother-of-Pearl handle.
Overall length 11" (279 mm).

"Heir To The Throne", 2002
Dagger, made of Five-bar Composite Damascus, 14k yellow gold (fused & fabricated), 22k yellow gold, 24k gold, emeralds, diamonds, sapphires, black opal and ivory handle. The Five-bar Composite Damascus blade was forged in 1995 under the direction of Master Bladesmith Rob Hudson.
Overall length 17 1/4" (438 mm).
From the collection of Dr. Thad Kawakami-wong, Hawaii.

Lloyd Hale
A pioneer of the Art Knife Movement

By Ed Wormser, USA

Lloyd Hale

Born in 1937 in Stillwater, Oklahoma, Lloyd became a full time knifemaker in 1969 at Poway, California. He became so well known for his Bowie knives that in 1973 the state of Arkansas recruited him and moved him to Springdale, Arkansas, with his wife and two children. Arkansas Parks and Tourism needed a Bowie knifemaker to create knives in the newly restored Blacks Forge, which is said to be the place where Jim Bowie had his famous Bowie knife made. It was here that Lloyd started doing file work on blades, and he is therefore credited with being the "Father of the Art Movement of the American hand-made knife".

In 1980 Lloyd moved his shop to Louisville, Kentucky, where he met Owsley Brown Frazier, a wealthy family member of the Kentucky Browns, known for their famous Kentucky Whiskey disttilleries. Frazier proposed that Lloyd create ONLY FOR HIM a one-of-a-kind knife collection. Lloyd had to drop off the map, attend no knife shows and show his work to no other knifemakers; and he was not allowed to look at knife publications so as not to be influenced by other people's work. For 23 years, Lloyd created this collection. In 2002 the collection was deemed complete and the knives were put into the Owsley Brown Frazier Antique Arms Museum of Lousiville, Kentucky.

Lloyd is now free to create knives for other collectors, and the two knives shown here are among his first creations since he gained his freedom.

When asked about returning to the Family of Knifemakers, Lloyd said, "I am really shocked and impressed by what I see being created today by custom knifemakers all over the world, but especially here in the States. I am so proud to have played a small part in all this..."

Opposite, from the left:
"Sub-Hilt Fighter", 2003
This magnificent Bowie is made of 440C stainless steel with nickel-silver bordering the Gold-Lip Pearl and abalone. Blade length 10 3/4" (273 mm), overall length 17 1/2" (444 mm). *From the collection of Ed Wormser, USA*

"Lapis Dagger", 2003
The blade and fittings are 440C stainless steel. Blade length 10 3/4" (273 mm), overall length 17" (432 mm). *From the collection of Walter Hoffman; USA*

San Francisco Knives

By Phil Lobred, USA

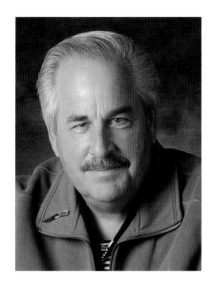

America became established only in the 1700s and therefore does not have the rich edged-weapon heritage of Europe or Asia. In 1800 most frontier knives were still imported and of repetitive shapes and materials.

The first American knife renaissance took place in San Francisco, California, during the gold rush of 1849. The magic word "gold" brought thousands of miners and immigrants, known as forty-niners, to the emerging-west-coast town of San Francisco. As the town grew into a city, it remained somewhat isolated from the products and influences of the more settled eastern part of the United States. With their newfound wealth these western pioneers not only coveted expensive things they also craved locally made products. They created their own style of life, a "San Francisco" style, consisting of fancy clothes, flashy guns and gear, fast horses and fine dress knives.

Beginning in about 1852, a number of very creative immigrant knifemakers set up shop in this artistically lacking environment. Makers like Hugh McConnell, Fredrick Kesmodel, Herman Schintz, Fred Will and Julius Finck (Will & Finck), Michael Price and others began to change the old lackluster styles. With the San Francisco elite both ready and able to buy, these makers created a new style of knife, a "San Francisco" style. These high quality dress knives for the discriminating had enough flash to satisfy the most ostentatious buyer. With their new shapes and use of such local products as silver and gold, carved ivory, abalone shell, engraving and silver sheaths, these knives sold for extraordinarily high prices for those times.

The competition among this brilliant group of makers resulted in the creation of some wonderful knife designs and fine workmanship. So creative were these knives, they are still being copied today.

T.M. DOWELL
BEND, OREGON

STEVEN J. RAPP
★ UTAH ★

B. WARENSKI
RICHFIELD, UT.

Opposite, from the left:
Contemporary San Francisco Knives
T.M. Dowel, Integral hilt construction with carved ivory handle. Carving and silver sheath overlay by Ron Skaggs.
Wolfgang Loerchner, California Ring Dagger with stainless steel and ivory.
Steven Rapp, Gold wrap and gold fittings with mammoth ivory inlays.
Buster Warenski, Carved mammoth ivory with silver fittings.

On the right:
Contemporary San Francisco Knives by Buster Warenski
Gold wrapped with gold fittings and gold bearing quartz inlays.
Silver wrap with abalone, Mother of Pearl, silver and gold.
Gold wrap and gold fittings and gold bearing quartz inlays.
Silver wrapped with silver fittings and African sugilite inlays.

Although much was written about these knives during their reign, less than 100 of the finest of them are known to exist today. America would not see a knife renaissance like this until the formation of the Knifemakers Guild in 1970. By the late '70s a new move to "art knives" was taking shape in the USA. As part of the new movement, makers such as Buster Warenski, Herman Schneider, Lloyd Hale, Jim Hardenbrook, Bob Oleson, T.M. Dowell and others began to recreate those magnificent knife designs of the 1800s - some in exact detail, some more contemporary, but all with the distinct "San Francisco" look.

These contemporary knives have superior workmanship, wonderful handle materials, carving, engraving, silver sheaths - and that traditional high price. Fitting the definition of an art knife these "period" knives, are now being created by some of the best knifemakers and engravers. Modern techniques and equipment make these new masterpieces superior to the antiques in fit and finish but they remain traditional in their "San Francisco" style.

Jim Kelso

The Knife Art of Jim Kelso

By Dr. Larry Marton, USA

Jim Kelso came to knifemaking in the late '70s with woodworking and self-taught engraving skills. He realized at that point that the easiest way to enter knifemaking would be to obtain ready-made blades to which he could apply his artistry. Early efforts included work with Rod Chappel and Phil Boguszewski. These early attempts were very instructive in gaining insights into knife design.

In 1980 Jim read an article in Esquire magazine on Damascus steel that mentioned Jimmy Fikes and Kemal (the team of Murad Sayen and Don Fogg). This article prompted Jim to visit several Damascus smiths, which convinced him to work only with forged blades. "I found the forged blade very appealing", Jim explained, "not only aesthetically, but also with regard to a most intriguing energy that was generated in talking to the smiths. Some embraced this work as a spiritual discipline. I thought long and hard about learning to forge Damascus but decided that, as an artist, I would have more than a lifetime of work to do in engraving and carving".

Don Fogg had recommended that Jim contact Jimmy Fikes, and this meeting led to his first collaborative Damascus knife. Fogg had also recommended that Kelso see the collection of Japanese swords at the Smith Museum in Springfield, MA. This was a pivotal experience for Jim, introducing him not only to the Japanese sword but to other Japanese decorative arts as well. Jim said, "I was blown away by the artistry I observed", said Jim, "I had previously never seen Japanese metalwork and my reaction to it was like a match set to tinder". Jim immersed himself in learning all he could about Japanese metalwork, visiting Japan on several occasions and obtaining grants from several prestigious foundations. His search for new knowledge continues until today.

Opposite, from the left:
"Kogatana", 1999 and **"Tanto", 1990**
Tanto and Kogatana blades in contemporary pattern-welded steel by Kiyoshi Kato. All other work by Jim Kelso. The kogatana is presented in a nontraditional way with it's own scabbard. The theme of the *kozuka* (handle) is the legend of Gamma-Sennin, an immortal who traveled with a three-legged toad. Gamma Sennin also was associated with the Peach of Immortality. Jim Kelso chose to depict the toad, who has lost his saintly companion and is desperate to reach the Peach of Immortality. The scabbard is made of wenge and ebony woods with mammoth ivory. The *kozuka* materials are silver, copper and gold. The tanto features a chrysanthemum theme with frog *menuki*. Commissioned by a Japanese collector.

On the right:
"Life and Death", 1997
The theme of this dagger (shown from both sides) is the opposing complimentary nature of life and death, the ultimate expression of opposites pairs. The mode of life is represented by an orchid in gold and silver, and an Australian boulder opal inset into the ebony handle. The mode of death is represented by a fierce demon in gold and silver, and chaotic pierced carving of the ebony. Carrying through the theme on the blade, Don Fogg has contrasted a beautiful feathery pattern in pattern-welded steel on one side (life) with a chaotic, textured surface of wrought-iron on the other (death). Kelso wished to convey the idea that although seemingly at odds, both life and death have an intertwined beauty and are inseparable parts of the whole.

About 1983, Jim met Louis Mills at the Knifemakers Guild Show in Kansas City, and they agreed to make a collaborative sword. At this point Louis had been making traditional Japanese blades for some time and, despite being self-taught, had made much progress. For the next 8 years or so, Jim worked almost exclusively with Louis Mills producing a number of elaborate Japanese-style swords, one of which was commissioned by the author and upon completion won the prestigious Cronk Award at the Knifemakers Guild Show. Jim reflected: "This was a particularly fruitful period, during which I developed my own engraving and design skills which were predominantly influenced by Japanese designs and works".

About 1990 Jim decided he wanted to work with blades that were not strictly Japanese. He met Phil Baldwin at the Guild Show and they agreed to make a piece together. Jim's love of winter's beauty inspired him to design the "Ice Dagger"; Phil made the blade, which Kelso hafted. This initial piece led to a number of further collaborations between Jim and Phil.

Around 1992, Jim and Don Fogg also began collaborating, and they have produced a number of unique pieces, including the "Life and Death Dagger' and the "Morning Glory Hunter".

It may be interesting to have some insight into the design process. According to Jim: "It seems to happen generally in one of three ways. A blade appears from a maker and I either like it or not. I design a package, including the blade, and ask one of the smiths if he would like to make it; or the smith and I work together on the design. Each of these approaches has its merits and potential difficulties, and all have worked equally well or not. There are many variables with each project, including collector input".

Jim feels there have been many benefits from his collaborative efforts over more than twenty years. "The rewards from collaborating in the knifemaking realm are varied. Certainly at the top of the list is the freedom that comes from not having to master yet another very demanding skill. Equally important, I have enjoyed the fellowship and the chance to work with and learn from some very accomplished artist/craftsman bladesmiths. There is something magically rewarding that emerges when people put their heads, hands and hearts together to reach a common goal".

Those of us who have had the privilege of owning a Kelso collaborative piece, or even of holding one in our hands and examining its incredible workmanship, understand the unique artistry that Jim brings to knife - and swordmaking. In a world of magnificent craftsmen, only the rare individual transcends the craft and elevates it to art. Jim is clearly one of the field's leading artistic and creative spirits.

"Maple Leaf" Tanto, 1986
"I first met Jim Kelso at the Anaheim Knife Show in 1985. Jim and Louis Mills were sharing a table, and Dr. Fred Carter insisted that I see their work. They were displaying an elaborately mounted Tanto which, unfortunately, had already been sold. Since an almost immediate affinity between Jim and I ensued, along with sincere admiration for his remarkable skills, the first of several commissions came into being. Jim and Louis completed this piece in time for the 1986 Knifemakers' Guild Show, where it won the W.W. Cronk Memorial Award for best knife in show.
I left all design considerations in Jim's hands, and he decided that the metal fittings should have an overall design of fallen maple leaves. They are cast in Sterling silver and finished with engraving and chasing, along with fused gold highlights".
The handle features both frog and cicada *menuki*, and has stingray skin under the silk wrapping. The *saya* (scabbard) is made from wenge wood with its grain enhanced by sand blasting and a lacquer finish. The *sageo* (fastening cord) was custom woven (*kumi-himo*) by Junko Narikawa.
Overall length 20 1/4" (513 mm).

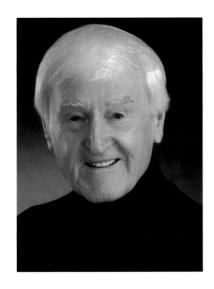

Classic Motifs in Modern Custom Art Knives

By Don Guild, Hawaii

CLASSIC. The term classic is from the Latin, meaning "the highest class". I consider "Classic motifs" to be art elements or themes, dating from before early Greek to Art Deco, of an excellence that never dies. For aeons man has produced artworks embellished with timeless themes and classic motifs. Today's knifemaker depicts his knife's "story" with historical exactness, or he personally interprets it. When he adds classic motifs and executes them with exceptional craftsmanship, his knife results in something timeless of "the highest class".

THE CANVAS. The custom art knifemaker's work differs from that of most other artist's, because the knifemaker starts by making an unadorned knife, whereas the artist does not make the canvas for his painting or the marble for his sculpture. I consider an unembellished knife "the canvas" to which the custom art knifemaker applies a classic motif or element. A superlative knife requires a demanding combination of skills, above and beyond bare execution, to produce a story comprising many layers of artistic innovation and meaning. The knife that ultimately turns out to be a classic is one where the knifemaker's artistic flair allows the final narrative to emerge. This assemblage of talent, from outset to finish, eventually tugs irresistibly at a collector's emotional side and demands his attention. But it all starts with the canvas.

THE MATERIALS. Materials found in fine museum swords and daggers dating back a thousand years are often seen in today's Classic Art Knives. Since the knifemaker can choose from a wide variety of materials, when he incorporates circa 1920 Bakelite for the handle of a classic Art Deco knife he makes use of a superbly appropriate material that yields true

authenticity; or when another maker embeds a river-washed ruby in the pommel of a circa 1450 replica dagger he also uses a tastefully of-the-period element to add a measure of authentic intrigue to his finished knife. There is no limit to the materials that can be used or the techniques that can be applied to create a classic Custom Art Knife.

THE TECHNIQUES. Knives can be fashioned using old and lasting techniques or be crafted using new and innovative techniques. I know of one maker whose knife reveals its story in an enchanting way when the he carves a "classic theme" on Titanium then anodizes it to elicit a technicolored eye-stopping handle; the result is charming and eclectic. Another knifemaker, by sculpting a Unicorn's horn from a narwhal tusk that he appliqués to a solid-gold Unicorn's head, also produces something organic and beautiful. So a knifemaker can add "Classic motifs" and choose a variety of techniques to free any special talent he has for sculpting, casting, carving, inlaying, coloring and/or engraving. Diverse techniques, when artfully executed, cement the knifemaker's art into a comprehensive message of classic appeal.

THE RESULTS. Today's collector seeks the extraordinary example to add to his collection, and collectors are captured by a knife embellished with an assemblage of "classic motifs". Although the right-brained collector gravitates toward a knife's fascinating story and its artistic virtues, machining and simplicity captivate the left-brained, engineering-type. Yet both types fall for the knife that is precisely made and further enhanced with those "classic motifs" that add history, charm, mystery and romance - qualities that give it intrigue and value for centuries to come.

Opposite:

"PERSEUS and MEDUSA" by Arpad Bojtos, 2002

Greek mythology tells how Perseus, the son of Zeus, killed the evil Medusa, who was so hideous, with her hair of hissing vipers, that all who looked upon her were turned to stone. The Goddess Athena gave Perseus a polished shield, Hermes presented him with a sword, and Mercury gifted him a pair of winged shoes to speed his journey. Perseus quietly approached the cave, where he found Medusa sleeping, and, while looking only at her reflection in his shield, he sliced off her head. Medusa's blood flowed to the sea, and from the froth emerged the magnificent white-winged stallion Pegasus, on whose back Perseus escaped. Arpad depicts this myth through his sculpting of gold, silver, steel, and snakewood, using only hammer and chisel. His interpretation of this renowned myth is exemplary.

The Elements of Blade Steels
The most important part of any knife... the part that cuts

By Deryk Munroe and bladegallery.com, USA

The principal alloying elements responsible for creating the final properties of a steel blade are: carbon, chromium, manganese, nickel, silicon, vanadium, molybdenum and tungsten. Sulphur, lead, copper, boron and phosphorous also play important, but less essential roles.

Carbon (C) is the basic element that allows a steel to become hard through the heat-treating process. No other element has a greater effect on the strength and hardness of a given steel as carbon. Small changes in the carbon content can greatly alter the performance of the final alloy. As a general rule, the maximum hardness of any grade of steel is attributable to its carbon content. The steels used by knifemakers generally contain between 0.5% and 1.5% carbon.

Chromium (Cr) is one of the three strongest carbide formers. It increases the depth of hardness and is the main element that gives a steel the ability to resist corrosion and oxidation. For a steel to be classified as stainless it must have a minimum of 13.0% chrome. Chromium is also a strong carbide former, and many steels rely on it to form their carbide matrix.

Manganese (Mn) is found in most steels as a deoxidizer and gives it the ability to be hot rolled or forged. Manganese also imparts responsiveness during heat treatment.

Nickel (Ni) increases the toughness and flexibility of the steel but does not increase the hardness. Also used to increase corrosion resistance.

Silicon (Si) is used for much the same reasons as manganese. Also used as a benefit for tensile strength and depth of hardness when used in combination with other elements.

Vanadium (V) is the second of the three main carbide formers. It is an expensive element to produce, but it is one of the most common elements used to increase the strength, hardness and wear-resistance of a steel. Vanadium carbides in a steel offer excellent resistance to abrasion, create a fine grain, and increase its edge-holding properties.

Molybdenum (Mo) is the third of the three strongest carbide formers. It is added to increase strength and ductility, and it greatly increases the depth of hardness. Molybdenum was not widely employed as an alloying agent until World War I, when it was used to toughen armor plating.

Tungsten (W) increases wear resistance and gives a tight, dense grain pattern to the steel. Tungsten (also known as wolfram), when used with chromium and molybdenum, can give a steel the property of "red hard", in which the steel will retain its hardness at high temperatures. These steels are often known as "high-speed steels".

Taking this basic alloying information and applying it to steels used in cutting-tool and knife-blade applications, we are presented with a world of trade-offs. All of the elements have both benefits and drawbacks. For instance, the more carbon in a given steel, the harder that steel can potentially become. But unfortunately, increased hardness = increased brittleness. In other words, a steel that is brought to maximum hardness would hold a sharp edge for a long time, but that edge (in fact, the entire blade) would be very fragile and susceptible to failure due to shock or flex. When discussing steels, hardness and strength are two different and distinct terms. Increase one and suffer a decrease in the other. Another example: The more chrome that is in a steel, the more rust-resistant that steel will be. But unfortunately, as the chrome content goes up, the steel becomes softer, "gummier", and more resistant to taking and holding a keen edge. Very small amounts of boron, ranging from 0.0005% to 0.003% percent increase the hardenability of steel without loss of ductility, the effect being most noticeable in steels with lower carbon levels.

ATS-34, to give one example, is one of the most famous and premium steels for cutlery blades. The alloying elements that create the final properties of this steel are: carbon 1.05%, manganese 0.25%, phosphorous 0.03%, sulphur 0.02%, chromium 14%, silicon 0.41% and molybdenum 4%.

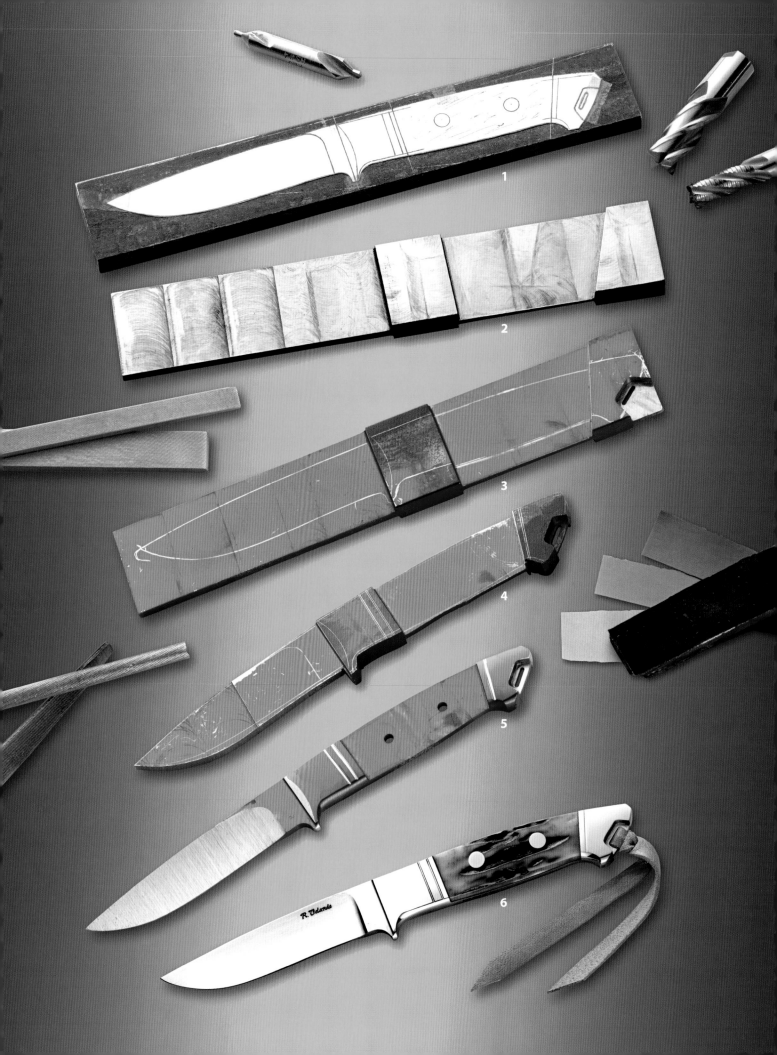

1

2

3

4

5

6

R. Velando

Integrals and Interframes

By Ricardo Velarde, USA

Integral and Interframe knives are made out of a single piece of steel. A "conventional" fixed-blade knife is usually made of 1/8" (3.2 mm) or 3/16" (4.8 mm) thick steel stock while everything else, such as the guard, is added on later. Integrals and Interframes, on the other hand, begin from 1/2" (12.7 mm) to 5/8" (15.9 mm) thick stock and are all one piece from the point of the blade to the end of the tang or pommel.

The process of creating a Full-Integral begins with deciding on the design for the knife and milling out the space for a 3/16" (4.8 mm) thick blade and a tapered tang, leaving the guard and pommel if included, full thickness. This is one of the simplest-looking knives, but technically it is the most difficult knife to make. The knife's profile is shaped using files, and a belt grinder is used to hollow grind the blade.

Semi-Integral knives include only a guard; **Full-integral** knives include a guard and a pommel; and **Interframe knives**, in addition, have pockets cut out on each side for inserting the handle material.

The Artists

Van Barnett
Charlie Bennica
Roger Bergh
Arpad Bojtos
David Broadwell
Dr. Fred Carter
Edmund Davidson
Jose de Braga
Jim Ence
Jerry Fisk
Larry Fuegen
Chantal Gilbert
Tim Hancock
Gil Hibben
D'Alton Holder
Paul M. Jarvis
John L. Jensen
S. R. Johnson
Dietmar Kressler
Francesco Pachì
Conny Persson
Pierre Reverdy
Scott Slobodian
Dwight L. Towell
Buster Warenski
Yoshindo Yoshihara

Pierre Reverdy (France) forging steel

Van Barnett
West Virginia, USA

Born in 1964 in Charlston, West Virginia, Van Barnett has been making knives full-time for twenty-four years, from the age of 17. He is a self-taught knifemaker and

started full-time after graduating from high school. Being an artist, he had thought of other artistic avenues, but knifemaking was a totally new way to experiment with his creativity. Van's artistic and creative capabilities go back as far as he can remember. He has always been an artist and has tried many different media through which to express his inner creativity. He is also a painter and a sculptor, as well as a carver. Van feels that:

"The creative mind soars endlessly, always questioning, always searching for new ways in which one can share what they have within with everyone else. That is the goal, to let people see life through your eyes and to share your dreams and visions, to give everything you create life - part of your life, something that will live on in the eyes and hands of others as they see and touch what you are. By touching the physical existence of your inward creativity they can see the beauty that you see and try to share in the world with everything you create".

So he goes on creating. Molding emotions into physical objects that people will share with each other long after he is gone. Van's knives are one-of-a-kind, with flowing designs and a three-dimensional look. Van believes strongly in sole authorship, therefore everything is done by himself alone, from forging his own Damascus to engraving, carving, gold work, and design. One of the greatest honors he has received is being voted into the Art Knife Invitational group (AKI). To be one of the 25 members of this group is an honor he cherishes. Van does high-end collector art knives and strives to make everything one-of-a-kind and truly unique.

Allowing the creative mind to flow and ask questions of the inner self permits answers from within to surface to a visible state. Now the eyes can see and partake of the true wealth of creative information that lies just below the surface of the conscious, revealing the dreams of our past and future in the realm of the subconscious mind.
This brings forth beauty in the things we create, because we tap into that never-ending source of our mind, the source for all our creations. To me, forming beautiful objects starts with an emotion that manifests itself into a physical presence through the eyes and hands of the artist. Once given its freedom into the real world, it is now able to stand on its own for all to see and feel.

Opposite:
"A Touch of Class", 1998
The most prominent feature in this dagger is the six sided Black-Lip Pearl handle with 14k gold fittings and embellishments and two diamonds. The four-bar Twist Damascus blade is beautifully hot blued and the hot blued mild steel guard and pommel are carved all the way.
Overall length 17" (432 mm).

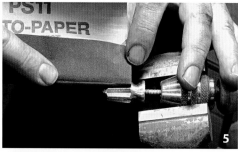

On the left:

Making a Fluted Pommel Without a Lathe

1 The tools Van uses to create pommels for his daggers are files, sandpaper, a drill chuck hand vice and a modified cordless screwdriver. The "raw" material for this pommel is a length of 3/4" mild-steel rod.

2 Van marks the center of the rod and rough grinds it to the desired shape on the corner of a one-inch-wide grinding wheel that is used only for this purpose, leaving enough of the flat surface on the steel to allow for it to be held in the vice for drilling.

3 Once the piece is shaped, it is then drilled and tapped to the needed thread size .

4 After drilling and tapping, the pommel is fitted with a short length of threaded rod and fixed onto the cordless screwdriver; it is then spun against the belt grinding wheel on the corners and on the flats to cut the grooves and create the desired shape and it is finished with belts of different grits.

This is how Van has always made round pommels for his daggers, finished looking as though they were made with a lathe. He used to spin the rod by hand, doing this until, about 13 years ago, knifemaker Doug Casteel suggested he use an electric drill, spinning the material much faster and truer than twisting it by hand, not to mention avoiding the finger cramps.

5 Filing the flutes into the pommel. This process is repeated with different grades of sandpaper to about 1000 grit till the pommel is ready for the buffing wheels.

6 The finished and polished pommel ready for hot gun bluing. Many different styles of round pommels can be made this way; it is the way Van started doing it over 23 years ago, and he still does it today, finding it hard to change old habits.

Opposite:

"Black Gold", 2004

Ladder pattern Damascus blade. Carved and hot blued guard and pommel. Fluted black ebony handle. 24k gold inlay and overlay on guard and fittings. Engraving on guard with 24k gold inlay. All work by maker. Overall length 16" (406 mm).

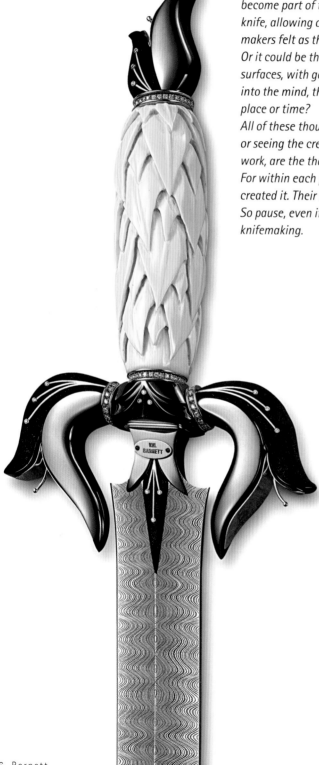

The HEART of Knifemaking

Within the pages of this book you will find many types of art in the form of knives. As you view each artist's work, take time and pause for a moment to view the artists themselves. As you do, you will see in them and their work a love and a passion for what they do with their own inner creativity.

To me, the creative energy that flows from us into what we create gives each piece an essence of the maker. It carries part of him or her within it for ever.

It may be in the smooth, comforting feel that makes the piece become part of the hand for daily use as a working or hunting-style knife, allowing one's mind to pause for a moment and feel what the makers felt as they created the knife for that specific purpose.

Or it could be the energy flowing from highly carved and engraved surfaces, with gold and gemstones, that soars up through one's arm into the mind, that allows one to dream for a moment of another place or time?

All of these thoughts and emotions which one feels from touching or seeing the creative energy that each maker puts into his or her work, are the thoughts and emotions of the artists themselves. For within each piece there remains a part of the individuals who created it. Their heart and their love of what they do.

So pause, even if just for a moment, and look into the HEART of knifemaking.

On the left:

"Garden of Eden", 1999

The blade is Ladder pattern Damascus and the elaborately carved handle is ivory. Carved and hot blued mild-steel guard and pommel, with texturing and 24k gold inlays. 124 diamonds are set in 14k yellow gold for a total of 3.4 carats. 14k yellow gold fittings and embellishments.
Overall length 19 1/2" (495 mm).

Opposite, from the left:

"Living Proof", 1997

The Ladder and Rosebud Damascus blade is nitre blued. Guard and pommel are mild-steel, carved and hot blued. Carved fossil walrus ivory handle, and carved roses in guard and pommel. 14k yellow gold fittings with 12 diamonds.
Overall length 18" (457 mm).

"Black Widow", 2000

Ladder pattern Damascus blade. Six-sided stone handle of pyrite and jet. Carved and hot blued mild-steel guard and pommel. All fittings and embellishments are 14k yellow gold.
Overall length 17 1/2" (444 mm).

"Jade Dream", 2001

Ladder pattern Damascus blade. Hot blued guard and pommel. 24k gold inlays with engraving on all sides. All fittings are 14k yellow gold.
Overall length 16 1/2" (419 mm).

Above:

"Poison Ivy", 1998

Ladder pattern Damascus blade. Carved fossil walrus
ivory handle. Hot blued mild-steel "D" guard and
pommel. 14k yellow gold leaves and vines. Eight
diamonds are set in 14k gold.
Overall length 16 1/2" (419 mm).

Opposite, from the top:

"Ivory Coast", 2003

Ladder pattern Damascus blade.
Hot blued mild-steel guard and
pommel. Carved ivory handle. All
fittings are 14k yellow gold. 24k
yellow gold inlays with engraving.
Overall length 16" (406 mm).

"Night Stalker", 2003

Persian-style dagger with a Ladder
pattern Damascus blade. Carved
ebony handle and hot blued mild-
steel guard and pommel. Engraving
on guard. 14k gold and 24k yellow
gold inlays.
Overall length 16" (406 mm).

Charles Bennica
Moulès et Baucels, France

Born in Sicily in 1949, Charles Bennica was 7 years old when his family emigrated to France. While still in school he began to make sketches of knives and he made his first dagger when he was 14 years old. Having qualified as a toolmaker he worked for a few years in the industry before creating his own precision tool making business.

At that time he was making knives just for his pleasure. However, in 1990, urged by a fellow knifemaker, he became a member of SICAC in Paris and discovered a whole new world of knifemakers and their art.

For the following six years he continued making knives, though still only as a hobby, and took part in several shows throughout Europe. At one of these he met Steve Johnson and Dietmar Kressler and was so excited by their work that he asked to spend some time in their workshops, learning how they achieved their flawless finish.

Creating his unique style right from the very first knife, he was inspired by the pure and simple line of the iris leaf. He used this design when making his first folding knife in 1991 as well as in the original shape of his butt cap closing mechanism.

In 1996, such was the demand for his knives, that Charles Bennica decided to sell his company and become a full-time knifemaker. Since 1996, he has participated in major shows in the USA and Europe.

In his free time he likes to ride on his motorbike (his first passion) or go shooting. He also has a passion for guns and found much inspiration for his knifemaking in their mechanical precision. But free time is a luxury that Charles cannot afford. Knifemaking occupies most of his day, with a waiting list of more than a year for new orders.

He believes that mechanical precision is akin to mathematics. It is either right or wrong, there is no "almost right". Quality, precision and reliability are and will always be his first priority.

Beginning as a collector, I soon realized that the actual making of knives was my true vocation, carrying out this craft, as I have been taught, in it's purest form. Designing a knife holds the same passion for me as making it. In the world of knife enthusiasts and collectors I have made wonderful friendships with both knifemakers and collectors, all speaking the same "knife language".
Some find the creative beauty of knives inspiring, for others it's their practical uses.
It's the fusion of both of these that fires my passion in the art of knifemaking.

Bennica

Opposite, from the left:
"Chrysalide miniature", 2002
Made as a gift for the Italian collector Pierluigi Peroni, this Integral-Interframe with Black-Lip Pearl inlays has a sculptured handle. The reverse side of the blade is marked "Pierluigi".
Overall length 4" (102 mm).
"Pearl Interframe", 2000
The smooth curves of this Integral-Interframe are complemented by the premium Mother-of-Pearl inlays.
Overall length 8 1/3" (212 mm).
"Chrysalide", 2001
An Integral-Interframe with sculptured handle and Mother-of-Pearl inlays.
Overall length 9 2/8" (235 mm).
All three knives from the collection of Dr. Pierluigi Peroni, Italy.

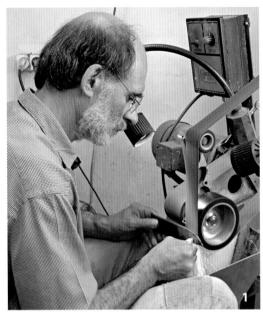

Making "New York", 2004

"I use various materials on the handles, looking for true beauty in the ivory, rare woods and Mother-of-Pearl, often using gold and semi-precious stones. For the blades I always choose high performance steel and Damascus steel from the most reputable smiths. Being a perfectionist, I push their tolerance to the limit and during the fabrication process insist on the strictest criteria for dimensions, finish and strength, achieving this with traditional machines and lots of files and sand paper".

1 Charles Bennica, grinding the outline of the blade.
2 Creating the bolster at the root of the blade, Bennica uses a hand-held file while turning the blade on the lathe.
3 The blade is held in the vice and finished by hand-working with sandpaper. Slowly using finer abrasives from number 600 grit to 1200 grit to reach the final result.

Opposite, from the right:
"New York", 2004

The bar of Damascus steel, made by Conny Persson (Sweden), is forged to shape and cut into two pieces - for the blade and for the heel of the knife. The final blade with its shaped bolster is shown with the piece of fossil walrus ivory that will be used for the handle.

The knife was Named "New York" after the first knife of this design, which won the Best Collaboration Award at the 1999 New York ECCKS. Overall length 8 7/8" (225 mm).

On the left:

"Les Gemeaux", 2003 and 2004

Two Integral-Interframes made from
Damascus bars by Conny Persson.
One with an Explosion pattern
Damascus the other with Twisted
Mosaic Damascus. Handles on both
knives inlaid with stabilized giraffe
bone.
Overall length of each 8 2/3"
(220 mm).

Opposite, from the left:

"Aigoual", 2004

Blade and heel made of Damascus
by Claude Schosseler (France).
The guard is stainless steel and
the handle stabilized giraffe bone.
Overall length 10 1/4" (260 mm).

"Duo D'Automne", 2004

Made of Damascus by Claude
Schosseler (France), both blades have
tool steel welded to the cutting edge
for especially good edge retention.
The handles are made of stabilized
poplar wood.
Overall length of each 9 13/16"
(250 mm).

Above:

"Couteau De L'Amite", 1999

This knife was created as a collaboration piece with Steve R. Johnson (USA) and named "Knife of Friends". Johnson made the blade while Bennica finished the handle with stabilized poplar wood. Overall length 8 13/16" (224 mm).

From the collection of Dr. Pierluigi Peroni, Italy.

Opposite:

"Le Sanglier", 2003

The blade of this beautiful hunting knife is ATS-34 steel, the handle made of aged elephant ivory scrimshawed by Aldo Rizzini. Overall length 10" (255 mm).

Roger Bergh
Bygdea, Sweden

Roger Bergh was born in Gothenburg, Sweden, in 1956. Although he grew up in a suburban environment, he spent his holidays with his grandparents on their farm. It was

these rural experiences that exposed him to knives, and he soon developed a passion for them. Even as a young boy, he began to collect knives. In 1970, at age 14, Roger began working with leather, and he later got in touch with the Lappish culture and its handcrafts, begining as a result to work with reindeer antlers as well.

In 1976 Roger studied traditional Swedish woodworking, root-basket weaving and country-style furniture making. Near this school was Sweden's largest cutlery factory, Mora Knives. Visiting the factory to buy some blade blanks - he finished the handles and sheaths himself - Roger met the owner, who showed him his vast private knife collection. From this point on, he was hooked. He began buying blades from different Swedish bladesmiths (very common in Scandinavia) and enjoyed using various materials to create the finished knife. While working mostly in the Lappish tradition, he felt the urge to find his own way. His fascination for biology and agriculture at this time (1977-94) led him to create one of Europe's largest ecological farms, raising

Roger (top) and Isak Bergh

organic crops. After all, he had a family to support. But he continued making knives during this period and at the beginning of the '90s discovered Damascus blades when he met Kaj Embretsen and Conny Persson. Roger bought blade blanks from Conny for a number of years before asking to be taught how to forge them himself.

Interested in spirituality and philosophy, as a part of expressing the fine arts, Roger always tries to integrate these aspects in his work. Art Noveau has always been a great inspiration for him and his son, Isak, who now does most of the figurative carving on his handles. He wants every knife to be a personal statement, a part of his life at that very moment.

What makes it so hard for me to resist knifemaking? The answer is simple, it has it all: The heat of the forge and the glow of hot steel. The beauty of the wood and ivory handles transformed into timeless sculptural art. The softness of the protective leather sheath and the wonderful people that I meet along the way... The knife has become an artform with few limitations, continuously brought to new levels but still inspired all along by thousands of years of tradition.

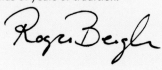

Opposite:
"Gold Dagger", 2003
This magnificent knife is a collaborative piece inspired by a sword displayed in a museum in Vienna, which belonged to Charles the Bold. Conny Persson made the Damascus billet, Roger did the grinding and carving of the blade and made the handle and Sara-mi Liljeholm did all the gold work and the rock crystal setting in the butt. The blade is 5-bar composite Twist pattern Damascus, forge-welded to the carved mild-steel section. Guard and spacers are high-carbon steel and nickel, with 18k gold in between. The handle is narwhal tusk wrapped in 18k gold. The knife won the award for Best Collaboration at the 2003 Atlanta Blade Show.
Overall length 11 1/2" (292 mm).

Carving the Blade

After drawing out the pattern of the planned design, the outline for the carving is cut on the roughly shaped blade. Various hand-held tools are used progressively, from the rough stages to the final perfecly finished carving of the 6" (152 mm) 3-bar composite Damascus blade.

Opposite:

"Captured Waves", 2004

The 6" (152 mm) blade is Bergh's 3-bar composite with Explosion pattern Damascus edge and back, and a center bar of very tight, twisted, end-cut multibar W-pattern steel with nickel stipes. The bolster is mammoth ivory bark in cross-section. The three-piece handle is of stabilized and dyed birch burl, fossil walrus tusk ivory (cross-cut) and Desert Ironwood. 23k gold insert in the blade.
Overall length 11 1/2" (292 mm).

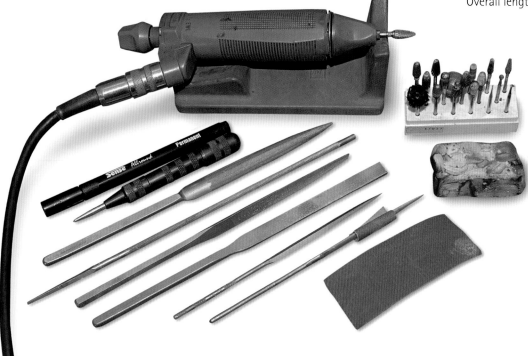

On the left:

"The Maiden", 2003

Six organic elements constitute the complex handle, which has been sculpted by Isak Bergh to partially reveal a beautiful maiden half-concealed behind those flowing locks of ivory, resulting in an aura of mystery. The 3-bar blade is created from Bergh's Explosion pattern Damascus made of 15N20 and 20C steel. This very well executed blend of the masculine hard steel and the softly sculpted femininity of the ivory handle result in a most harmonious statement. Carved maiden material is warthog tusk, tan filler is whale tooth, wood filler is Desert Ironwood, ring material is mammoth ivory.
Overall Length 9 3/4" (248 mm).

Opposite:

"Norse Gods", 2003

Roger's dagger is gracefully sculpted end to end. The metaphysical carvings are of Norse deities and depict Thor, the god of thunder, on one side of the handle and the goddess of life on the other. The old and the older blend, in the one-hundred-year-old flowing organic Art Nouveau style in which the carving is done and the deities of a thousand years ago. The continuity of the sculptural Nouveau bas-relief handle continues to the guard and throughout the blade. Blade, guard and bolster are 15N20 and 20C steel, spacers are 18k gold, and the handle, sculpted by Isak Bergh, is killer whale tooth from the 1920s.
Overall Length 10" (254 mm).
Both knives from the collection of Don Guild, Hawaii.

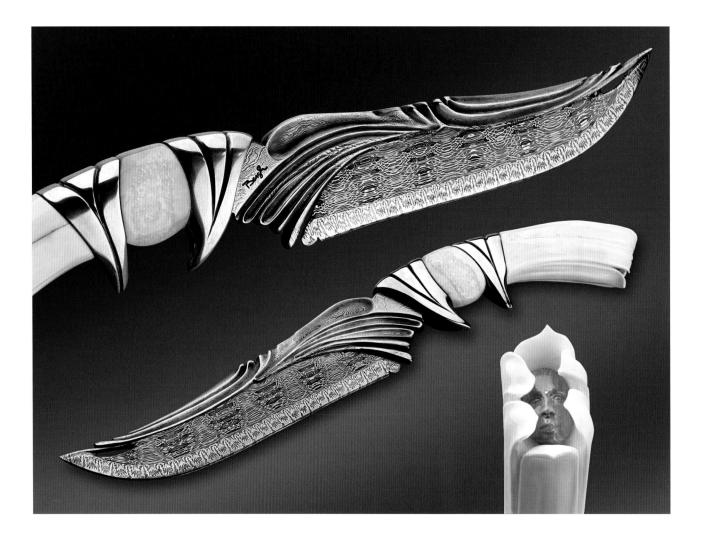

Above:

"Hidden Spirit", 2003
The blade is carved out of a 2-bar steel billet. The back bar is accordion-cut Mosaic Damascus and the edge is made of Explosion pattern Damascus. The sub-hilt guards are carved of mild-steel. The middle section of the handle is a walrus ivory artifact cross-cut, the end section is warthog tusk. The carved face in the "floral" end of the handle is made of chocolate-brown mammoth ivory. Overall length 12" (305 mm).

Opposite, from the top:

"Open D-Guard", 2004
The blade is 3-bar composite W-twist Firecracker pattern Damascus. The bolster, guard, butt cap and loop are all Random pattern nickel-steel Damascus. Name plate and spacers are silver.
Overall length 13 1/2" (343 mm).

"Dragon Fire", 2004
The blade is 3-bar Explosion and Twist pattern Damascus. Carved sub-hilt guards are mild-steel. Mammoth ivory handle carving was designed by Roger and done by his son, Isak Bergh. It was inspired by Native American designs, Chinese kon-fu-tse and ancient Eastern mythology. Overall length 13 1/8" (333 mm).

Arpad Bojtos
Slovakia

Arpad Bojtos was born in 1956 in the southern part of what is now Slovakia. After finishing his studies in economics, he was employed in various state companies in the former Czechoslovakia. Most of his free time was spent visiting museums and art galleries or painting and woodcarving, which had been his main hobby since childhood. Given the lack of space at home and the high cost of materials, he had begun to do lino-cut graphics and had replaced the big pieces of wood with pieces of bone, which he carved in his kitchen just for his wife's satisfaction.

In 1983, while on a business trip to Damascus (Syria), he found the time as usual, to visit several museums and was confronted with a great number of exquisite oriental knives and daggers. Later, while wandering among antique shops, he found many attractive pieces of cutlery that he regretfully could not afford, as he had just bought a family house. Not having the extra money for his new passion, Arpad decided to put his hobby to work and create similar objects for his own pleasure. He made his first knife three years later, in 1986.

Arpad has kept on making knives ever since, his hobby becoming a full-time obsession only in 1989, after the fall of communism. In 1991 he began to participate actively in several European knife shows and, begining in 1995, began visiting some of the American shows too. In 1996 he became a member of the Knife Makers Guild.

Bojtos creates all his knives as one-of-a-kind arworks; no two pieces are ever the same. He uses hand tools exclusively for stock reduction and carving, and his favorite tools still remain the hammer and chisel. Carving steel by hand is so time consuming that Arpad can make no more than 8 knives per year. He also carves the steel blades, preferring to work with ATS-34 or 440C when making fixed-blade knives. For his folders he often uses Damascus steel. Having made over one hundred knives to date, Arpad likes to use themes based on various classic and historic events, mythology, nature and exotic cultures.

When I made my first knife I intended to carve the handle and sheath myself as I had much practice from years of bone carving. I used a stag antler for the handle, but asked a gun carver to decorate the blade for me using my drawings. Luckily for me he refused to do this, as he had never carved human figures before. One of my friends, Julius Mojzis, a blacksmith, knifemaker and engraver, advised me to try carving the steel myself. He also showed me how to sharpen the chisels for working on steel and for carving silver and gold. That was all the pushing I needed.

Opposite:
"Column Dagger", 2003
This knife was made to honor the memory of ancient Rome. The steel used for the knife and the she-wolf is 440C, the capital is made of silver with gold acanthus leaves. The handle is made of ivory. The sheath is also made of ivory combined with black buffalo horn and silver and gold fittings.
Overall length 12" (305 mm).
From the collection of Don Guild, Hawaii.

Making the "Indian Buffalo Hunter"

After creating the rough shape of the knife, the steel is heated to a temperature of 860°C for 45 minutes to obtain the relative softness needed for carving. Bojtos doesn't like to use vices, so he uses the pitch-pan to hold the blade steady while carving. He first carefully plans the designs, and then draws them on the steel using felt-tip markers. A rough carving of the relief is made with hammer and chisels. The relief is then "cleaned" using files and scrapers, and Arpad proceeds to carve in the fine details. Finally the three-dimensional picture is cleaned out and finished using sandpaper and grinding pastes. After heat treating the steel, Arpad fixes the handle slabs to the knife with 14k gold pins.

Arpad spends a great amount of time researching a subject and begins to visualize the design for a knife long before he actually starts working on it. He sketches again and again while discussing his designs with his wife, Daniela, and daughter, Zuzana, who are his first and severest critics. It sometimes takes him months, even years, before he makes the final drawings for a new knife. Only then does he begin to choose suitable materials for the handle and sheath. It is an unwritten rule with Arpad not to use walrus or narwhale ivory for a tropical design or exotic woods and elephant Ivory when carving an arctic scene. Old trees are often a dominant feature in his carving, as his work space overlooks the town's park, with many of its hundred-year-old trees in full view.

Opposite:

"Indian Buffalo Hunter", 2004

A Semi-Integral made of 440C steel. The handle material is cocobolo wood, and the sheath is made of one piece of hollowed-out cocobolo wood, with silver fittings darkened by sulphuric acid. The buffalo skulls on the sheath are carved mammoth ivory. Overall length 9 1/4" (240 mm). *"For this knife, as I often do for my knife carvings, I chose a theme related to native tribes and their association with the surrounding wildlife. Since I like to combine both human and animal elements, I think this is a typical knife of mine".*

Above:

"Captain Cook", 1998

An Integral knife made of ATS-34, which is
a very suitable material for fine carving. The
handle is of mammoth ivory. The ivory globe
can rotate. The sheath is made of stingray
skin and has carved silver fittings.
Overall length 9 7/16" (240 mm).

Opposite, from the right:

"Jaguar Hunter", 1999

The steel for this Semi-Integral is 440C stainless steel.
The handle material is mammoth ivory carved and
combined with ebony. Dots on the jaguar are inlaid
with ebony pins. The sheath is made of stingray skin
and has carved silver fittings.
Overall length 7 7/8" (200 mm).

"Perseus Fighter", 2000

This deeply carved Semi-Integral is made of 440C.
The handle and sheath materials were chosen to
accentuate the snakes on Medusa's head, held
high in the hand of Perseus. The handle material is
snakewood and the sheath is made of snakewood
partly covered with snake skin, silver fittings and a
gold snake.
Overall length 7 7/8" (200 mm).

"Chameleon", 2002

The blade is ATS-34. The handle and the sheath are
made from moose antler. The sheath with silver
fittings is partly covered with ostrich skin.
Overall length 7 7/8" (200 mm).

On the left:

"The Snail Hunter", 2004

A Semi-Integral, made of 440C steel.
The handle material is carved moose
antler, the sheath is made of moose
antler, stingray skin, silver and 14k
gold. Overall length 7 7/8" (200 mm).
"Sometimes I like to choose a subject
that depicts smaller living creatures,
rather than carving "big game"
animals like lions and elephants.
These are quite often living creatures
that can be found and studied in my
garden, at home. One such animal is
the tiny snail I chose as the subject
for my three dimensional carving
on the steel of the blade and on the
handle material. For the sheath I
chose to carve a small frog".

Opposite, from the right:

"The Unicorn", 2002

Arpad used narwal ivory for both
handle and sheath, physically
connecting this knife to the medieval
legend of the Unicorn that is carved
on it. Damasteel was used for the
blade, and stingray skin combined
with silver and gold fittings complete
the ivory sheath.
Overall length 12 1/2" (317 mm).

"Gazelle", 2003

The deeply carved steel is ATS-34.
The boxwood for the handle
and sheath were something of
a challenge, as in the Middle Ages it
was very popular as a handle material
in Central Europe. The sheath is partly
covered with ostrich skin and has
silver fittings combined with gold.
Overall length 9 7/16" (240 mm).

David Broadwell
Texas, USA

Born in 1954, David Broadwell lives in North Texas. As a young boy, David was enamored with armor and weaponry in the hands of noble warriors. He used his imagination, a bathrobe for chain mail, a cardboard shield and his great-grandfather's Masonic sword to "slay the dragon". Bearing the brunt of his courageous attack was a mimosa tree in the front yard! His youthful interest in knives was rekindled in his twenties. After studying Criminal Justice in college, he worked as a machinist. Picking up a worn shop file, his first attempt at grinding a knife in 1981 gave him a chill from head to toe and he thought, "I have got to do this for a living!" Fellow knifemaker, the late Bob Hajovsky, worked in the same shop and was a great source of encouragement and information. By 1989 Broadwell had left the machine shop and was making knives full-time. Large fighters, sub-hilts and bowies were followed by flowing daggers, elegant folders, more sculpting, texturing and patinas. By the mid-1990s his work was firmly focused on "art knives".

His knives are known for their flowing, organic lines, textural carving, sculpting and meticulous fit and finish. In an age of high tech production, Broadwell's work is still done individually as an artist-craftsman, primarily one-of-a-kind commissioned pieces. Even limited editions are ground, fit, and finished by hand. He works directly with private collectors and a few select art knife purveyors. Broadwell also makes one-of-a-kind fountain pens with the same level of artistic expression and many of the patterned metals and materials he uses in his art knives.

It is a challenge for me to create knives that are recognized for their own artistic beauty and value, rather than simply becoming nicely crafted canvases for other artists to embellish, all the while maintaining their basic function as a fine tool. Making knives is a wonderful creative outlet, giving me much personal satisfaction as an artist; and being able to provide for my family as a professional knifemaker, a dream that first came to light in 1981, makes it even better!

David Broadwell

Opposite, from the left:
"Jade Dagger", 2002
One of Broadwell's free-form daggers fully sculpted in his organic style. The blade is made from a billet of Nick Smolen Damascus in a variation of his "Smoke" pattern. *"The result of Nick's forging and my grinding gave this knife a pattern that reminded me of Van Gogh's painting 'Starry Night'"!* The bronze fittings and the British Columbian nephrite jade handle are also deeply sculpted.
Overall length 15" (381 mm).

"Integral Sub-Hilt Fighter", 2003
"This is one of my favorite designs. I've felt that everything came together just right in it". Broadwell took a single large piece of steel to form the guard/sub-hilt fitting, then fitted the finely figured walnut handle material into it. Ray Cover, Jr., engraved the fitting and inlaid it in fine gold. The blade was ground from 154CM stainless steel.
Overall length 14" (355 mm).

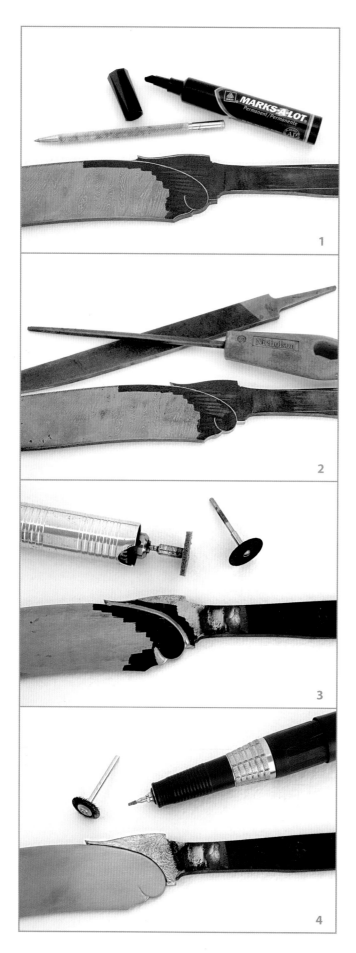

On the left:

Carving the Blade

1 The blade has been laid out and rough-ground to shape. Note that material has been left at the detail areas around the rear of the blade. Broadwell finds that an ink marker is very useful for quick layout.

2 Various files are used to finish the perimeter of the blade. In this case, a triangular file and a knife-style file are used. The re-curved element at the upper rear has been shaped with the smaller wheels on the belt grinder. The blade is ready for rough grinding and heat treatment.

3 After heat treatment the blade is ground to size and taken to a fairly high level of finish, then laid out again for final carving. A rotary tool is used first with the abrasive cut-off wheel to "cut in" the grind line and ricasso area, which are then smoothed to shape, connecting the upper and lower elements and blending them into a harmonious line.

4 Using a smaller high-speed rotary tool and a diamond burr, the ricasso is textured. Diamond is used because all the decorative work has been done on a hardened blade, but carbide or steel burrs can be used before heat treatment. A wire brush is put in the rotary tool and the textured area is burnished. The blade is ready to be fitted with its handle and etched to show the Damascus pattern. The textured area will be masked off to prevent it from etching in the acid.

Opposite page:

"Fighter", 2004

The Damascus blade is from Nick Smolen's Turbulence multi-bar pattern. After etching the steel to bring out the pattern, the blade is blued, then hand polished to highlight the pattern. The fittings are silicon bronze. The texturing is not random but is planned to follow the sculpting. The handle is polished ebony with asymmetrical carving and texturing. A three-leaf design can be seen carved into the finial. *"I think finials are very important in the design of an art knife, so on many I carve extra details into them. Otherwise, they are simply a mechanical device that holds the knife together, nothing more".* Blade length 10" (254 mm). Overall length 15 1/4" (387 mm).

Above:

"Sculpted Hunter", 2001

This knife is similar to one Broadwell actually carried on hunting trips. Raindrop pattern Damascus steel from Nick Smolen was used for the blade, which was carved with leaves and highlighted with texturing on the ricasso. The bronze fittings and Mediterranean briar handle have also been sculpted and textured. Instead of the more common etching or stamping, the blade mark has been carved in raised relief.
Overall length 9" (228 mm).

Opposite, from the left:

"Sculpted Persian Knife", 2004

This knife illustrates Broadwell's organic style of sculpting with detail carving on all major components of the knife. The 9 1/2" (241 mm) blade is made from Smolen Twist pattern Damascus, with carving on the ricasso. The area between this carving and the bevels has been relieved and textured, then burnished and left bright, while the surrounding Damascus has been etched to show the pattern. The guard and false tang are fabricated from bronze. The handle scales are fossil mammoth ivory. The two pins are bronze with textured heads, and the knife is finished with a medallion on the ricasso bearing Broadwell's blade mark.
Overall length 14 1/2" (368 mm).

"Pearl Bowie Knife", 2000

Typical of Broadwell's Bowies, this classic knife has a 10" (254 mm) blade of Smolen fine-layered, Ladder pattern Damascus. It is flat ground with a distal taper. The guard and the fabricated false tang handle frame and bolsters are made from Twist pattern Damascus. The false tang is carved in an unraveled rope pattern, and the fittings have a blued finish. The handle scales are white Mother-of-Pearl attached with gold pins. *"I find the occasional Bowie knife a pleasure to make. In my mind, Bowies form a link to an historical past".* Overall length 15" (381 mm).

"Sculpted Sub-Hilt Fighter", 2004

This knife shows a moderate level of sculpting. The 10" (254 mm) blade is made from Smolen Twist pattern Damascus, and is flat ground with a sweeping grind line at the rear. This grind line is profiled in a flowing organic shape and is "cut in" where it meets the ricasso. The ricasso is textured, with the texture pattern flowing out of the upper rear corner as if it were growing from under the fittings. The front collar, the guard and sub-hilt piece, and the finial are made from heat-colored bronze. The handle material is made of stabilized jarrah wood, and it has been fitted into the guard unit. Overall length 15 1/4" (387 mm).

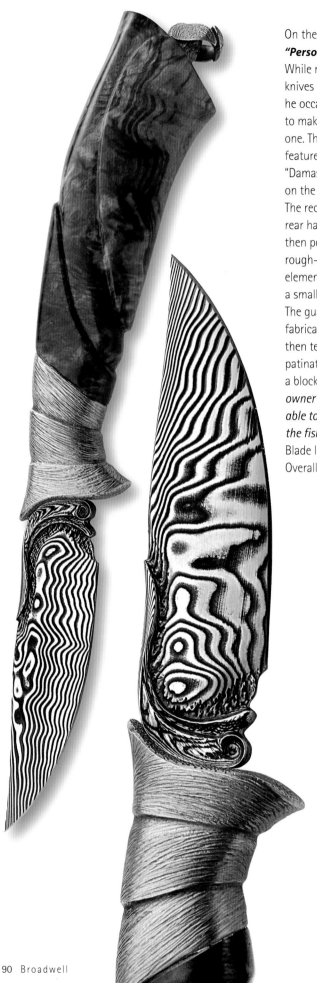

On the left:

"Personal Knife", 2004

While most of Broadwell's fixed-blade knives tend to be on the large side, he occasionally has the opportunity to make smaller ones such as this one. This "bird and trout" sized knife features a blade from stainless "Damasteel" with fine detailed carving on the ricasso and along the spine. The recurved scroll along the upper rear has been very lightly etched then polished. The spine ahead of it is rough-textured and etched. The scroll elements at the rear are textured with a small tool, then moderately etched. The guard and finial with bale are fabricated and carved from bronze, then textured, burnished and lightly patinated. The handle is carved from a block of rhododendron burl. *"The owner of this knife asked that it be able to disassemble for cleaning after the fishing trip!"*
Blade length is 2 5/8" (67 mm). Overall length 6 3/4" (171 mm).

Opposite, from the left:

"Engraved Persian", 2004

You will see here a resemblance to other Persian style knives Broadwell has created, with the slightly upturned point and the dropped handle. This one, however, shows how Broadwell and engraver Ray Cover, Jr., work closely together to create a collaborative piece of art. The bronze guard has been engraved in an elegant flowing scroll work that typifies Ray's work. Other features of the knife include a Twist pattern Damascus blade with carved scroll and textured background at the ricasso. Close examination shows that the texture forms a pattern and is not simply random. Broadwell carved the small bronze inserts in a three-leaf pattern. The handle is red mallee wood from Australia, and the maker's mark is cast into the silver disk that is part of the pin.
Blade length is 9 1/2" (241 mm). Overall length 14 3/4" (375 mm).

"Sculpted Dagger", 2004

This knife is a new design from Broadwell. The "guard" is in part integral with the blade, with a separate central fitting. The Twist pattern Damascus blade is ground from a heavy billet. Broadwell started with a piece of steel almost 7/16" (11 mm) thick, carved the rear area, then ground the bevels first with an 8" (203 mm) diameter wheel then with a 1 1/2" (38 mm) wheel. This technique gives the deep hollow-ground effect with a thick center ridge. The fittings are silicon bronze, carved with various textures and patinated. The handle is fossil walrus ivory with asymmetrical carving. The bronze finial is fitted with a domed cabochon of fossil ivory. *"While this knife has complexities in its design, I laid it out from a simple gentle arc".* Blade length is 8 1/2" (216 mm), overall length 13 1/2" (343 mm).

Dr. Fred Carter
Texas, USA

Born in 1940, Dr. Fred Carter has had a long-standing passion and interest in handicrafts, in particular, knives. In 1973, while studying for a Ph.D. in Botany in Arizona, he admired a hand-made knife by D'Alton Holder in a local knife shop. Inspired by this knife he decided to make hunting knives for himself and his father. These first knives were ground on a hard wheel and hand-finished. Upon their completion Fred received an offer to purchase one of his knives, and this was the start of his career in knifemaking. Later he began working in a small shop in Scottsdale, Arizona, before moving to Texas.

In 1976 Carter joined the Knifemakers Guild, in which he later served as secretary, treasurer, vice president and two terms as president.

Dr. Carter has won many awards for his knives, including the W.W. Cronk Award (1988, 1989) for best knife of the Knifemakers Guild Show and the Beretta Award for craftsmanship. His style is often as simple as possible, with sleek flowing lines complemented by engraving and gold work. His knives are all sole authorship, including all engraving and gold work. Prior to 1991 his main area of focus was fixed-blade knives, hunters, Bowies, daggers and fighting knives, many of which were highly decorated, along with many utility designs. Since 1991 he has concentrated on folding knives, which are embellished with engraving and gold. Carter has also done many Integral fighters and hunters, along with knives cast in dendritic 440C steel from injection molds of his own design and construction. Since 1995 he has joined forces with the Gigand Co. Ltd. and the United Cutlery Corporation to design and market high-quality production knives. Carter has designed knives for the Harley-Davidson Co., Colt, UZI, Browning, Remington, Ford Motor Co. and several other brands. He is most proud of being the designer of the 100th anniversary knives for Harley Davidson. Presently he continues to design production knives and make hand-made knives at his shop in Texas.

I was introduced to this craft in 1973 and it has occupied my thoughts and actions on a daily basis ever since. The late knifemaker Jim Schmidt once told me that the most wonderful thing about this craft is that it is never-ending. That was an understatement. On many levels, it is much more than just a craft. This craft can, in a way, consume you, and the knives become a part of you, they are your children, your legacy, your gift to future makers and collectors. These wondrous objects come to life right before your eyes, often to your amazement and surprise. I feel that this is my destiny and I have pursued it with all my passion and strength; this is not a hobby, it is serious business. I can honestly say that this craft has been good to me and I have been good to it, what more could one ask? I will continue to design for production, make custom knives and look forward to what the future will hold.

Opposite, from the left:
"AKI Bowie", 1997
Flat ground 440C stainless steel hand-finished blade. Handle is 1018 low carbon steel engraved and gold inlaid. Relief gold borders around the edges of the guard and handle tang. Hot blued fittings with the scroll engraving done in French gray. Overall length 8 1/2" (216 mm).

"Ivory Handled Fighting Knife", 1984
Hollow ground 440C hand-finished blade. The handle is elephant ivory with engraved 416 stainless steel fittings. Overall length 7 1/4" (184 mm).

"English Style Bowie", 1998
Flat ground 440C hand-finished blade. Low carbon steel fittings with relief engraving and gold inlay. Polished elephant ivory handle. Overall length 8 1/2" (216 mm).

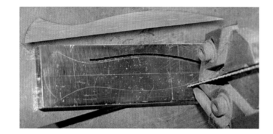

On the left, from the top:

Making the Darom Dragonfly Dagger

The Darom dagger began as two pieces of raw steel, one block of 1018 low carbon and one bar of Starrett brand high carbon O-1 steel. Starrett steel is the preferred steel, as it is consistently pure and polishes like a mirror. The low carbon block was first squared by milling and then drilled to a predetermined depth based on the blade depth into the handle. The block was then slit to the depth needed to intersect the drilled hole, allowing the blade steel to slip into the handle and butt against the back of the slit. The outline of the handle was scribed on both sides of the handle block. The block was then roughly sawn to shape, and excess material was ground away right up to the outlined handle. The blade was made in the same manner. The back edge of the blade was milled square while leaving the tang material in the center; the tang was then filed until it would slip into the hole drilled into the handle. The handle surface was rough ground to shape on the belt grinder and then brought to final shape by filing and draw-filing the surface to produce a curved upper surface. The blade was also marked and roughed out on the belt grinder, then filed and draw-filed to its final shape. Both the handle and the blade were hand-sanded to a 320 grit finish, and the engraving design was sketched onto their surfaces. The rough decoration was then drawn with a metal scribe and the scribed lines cut lightly into the surface with the graver. Next the engraved outlines were deepened and the linear leaves cut deeper, scooped out and undercut to hold the silver that would be inlaid. Once the silver was in place the entire handle was sanded using finer and finer sandpaper until it began to shine. At this point 8000 grit diamond paste was applied and rubbed until a mirror finish was obtained. The final finish was with 14,000 grit diamond paste. Once polished, the scroll engraving on the butt was detailed; no polishing or sanding was done once engraved as sanding or polishing will take the glisten off of the edges of the engraving and shading, making it look dull. The next step was to add the dragonfly overlay. The gold overlay was attached by criss-cross cutting the surface with a flat graver. This criss-cross cut kicks up small burrs on the surface that imbed into the soft 24k gold wire, holding it securely. After the area has been covered with wire it is hammered into a solid-appearing surface. The gold is then cut, trimmed and detailed to give a more life-like appearance to the dragonfly. The blade was polished to a 2000 grit finish, engraved and heat treated. After heat treatment it was again sanded with 2000 grit and polished to a mirror finish with diamond paste. The parts were then hot blued to protect the metal and show the gold and silver work. The handle and blade were then slipped together and secured with the pommel nut.

"The final dagger is as you see it. It was a pleasure to make for my good friend David and this book".

Opposite:

"DDD-2" Dragonfly dagger, 2004

An all-steel dagger with a 5 7/8" (149 mm) blade. The hand shaped O-1 steel blade has been relief engraved and diamond polished. The handle into which the blade is fitted has been hand polished, relief engraved with scroll and inlaid with silver. The main decorative element is a gold dragonfly which is done in 24k gold overlay. The entire knife has been given a hot blued finish. The dagger is seen here with a matching folder made by Fred in 2002 for the book *"Art and Design in Modern Custom Folding Knives".*
Overall length 9 1/4" (235 mm).

On the left:
"AKI All-Steel Dagger", 1993
Double flat ground 9" (228 mm) blade of laminated Japanese stainless steel given to Dr. Carter by Akahisa Kawasaki. The handle, guard and pommel were made from low carbon steel, relief engraved and inlaid with 24k gold scroll done in relief. The handle was hot blued to further enhance the gold work. Overall length 14 1/2" (368 mm).

Opposite, from the left:
"Ivory Engraved Dagger", 1987
The 9" (228 mm) blade, made of 0-1 steel, was asymmetrically hollow ground, hand-finished and gold and silver inlaid with morning glory flowers and vines. The spiral fluted elephant ivory handle is wrapped with 14k twisted gold wire. The guard was hand-forged to shape from low carbon steel. All of the knife fittings along with the blade were hot blued.
Overall length 14 1/2" (368 mm).
"Ivory Engraved Dagger", 1987
The 9" (228 mm) blade, made of 0-1 steel, was double flat ground, relief engraved and gold inlaid. The fittings are of low carbon steel that has been inlaid with vines and flowers, and features 24k gold butterflies done in relief. The elephant ivory handle has been spiral fluted and wrapped with 14k twisted wire.
Overall length 14 1/2" (368mm).
Both knives from the collection of Don Guild, Hawaii.

Above:

"AKI All Steel Dagger", 1999

The 6" (152 mm) blade is made of O-1 steel, hand-shaped by draw-filing then hand diamond polished with relief engraving and gold inlay. The handle is low carbon steel and was hand shaped by filing. The handle was then hand polished with diamond paste after being engraved and gold and silver inlaid with morning glories; lastly it was adorned with relief-sculpted 24k gold butterflies.

Opposite:

"Three Miniature Bowies", 1996

These bowies were designed after the famous I*XL California Style knives of the 1850s. The uppermost Bowie is an all-steel knife with 24k gold inlay and blued steel fittings. The center Bowie is fitted with engraved stainless steel fittings and Gold-Lip Pearl handle inlays held with gold pins. The bottom Bowie features stainless steel fittings, relief engraving and Gold-Lip Pearl handle inlays. All three knives have 440C stainless steel heat treated blades and true relief scroll engraving. Overall length of each knife is 4 1/2" (114 mm).

Edmund Davidson
Virginia, USA

Born in 1954 near Goshen, Virginia, Edmund Davidson was privileged to have been raised on his family's 2,000 acre estate. Having grown up in the farmhouse built by his grandfather in 1886 helped forge Edmund's appreciation for history, past and future. At the age of 11 his mother insisted he take piano lessons, and this was the beginning of his eye-hand coordination and his first introduction to the arts. Two years later, his father bought him a lapidary machine and he began making rock jewelry and, later, rifle stocks and pistol grips, further honing his eye-hand skills. In 1969 he was introduced to two Bob Loveless drop-point hunting knives owned by visiting hunters, and he was hooked on handmade knives forever.

In 1975 Edmund began a career as a cross-country long-haul trucker, fulfilling a childhood dream and forging his character from lessons learned and knowledge gained on the road. In April 1986 Edmund began knifemaking full-time and with a wealth of determination, making another dream come true.

Photographs published in the mid 1970s had a profound impact on his life as a knifemaker, inspiring him to adopt the integral methods of knife construction.

"My first impression of those early knives was that they were of a truly novel concept. Here was a knife that completely eliminated solder joints, gaps and vulnerable areas where stress risers could develop. Since my humble beginnings as a knifemaker in 1986, I have developed over 90 unique integral patterns, which include several designs from the shop of R.W. Loveless. From virtually indestructible camp and combat knives to many highly functional hunting knife patterns and investment-quality embellished art pieces, I will continue to push the proverbial integral envelope and develop new patterns for as long as I am able".

Influenced by Bob Loveless, T. M. Dowell and, Billy Imel, Edmund developed his own style, one that has clearly set him apart in the world of custom knifemaking.

I consider the modern fixed-blade knife to be mankind's "ultimate hand tool". No other time in world history have knives around our planet been made so well and with such remarkable materials as they are in our time. Knifemakers at present are in a league all by themselves. They are artists and craftsmen making the age-old knife their way, as they see it. Few items in all of history have endured to become what handmade knives are today.
My wish is for handmade knives in the future to exceed what we make now, so in all things, "build today for many tomorrows".

Edmund Davidson

Opposite, from the left:
"Sheffield Bowie", 2002
Three years in the making (1999-2002), this all Integral Bowie was made of A-2 steel, heat treated by Paul Bos and hardened to 58 Rc. The blade is flat ground, filed and hand rubbed to a 600 grit finish all over. Engraving by Jere Davidson and the ivory handle scrimshawed by Linda Karst Stone.
Overall length 17" (432 mm).
"Buffalo Bowie", 1996
"This is the most spectacular knife I have worked on. An art collector commissioned it in 1995 and I feel honored to have been selected for the project". Made of 440C steel, this all Integral Bowie was heat treated by Paul Bos to 58 Rc. The handle is Elephant ivory. Engraving by Jere Davidson.
Overall length 13 1/4" (336 mm).

1

On the left:

"Max's Fancy Hunter" in the Making

"My knives are all made in my shop with my equipment. I purchase my blade steel in the form of bar stock and the mechanical fasteners that I use to attach handle materials."

1 The rough bar of BG-42 steel made by "Latrobe Steel" is 1/2"x1 1/2"x 8 1/2" (13x38x216 mm).

2 The milling machine is now used to square up the butt cap end of the steel bar after the rough sides have all been milled level and square.

3 Using a #2 Cincinnati milling machine built in 1938, Edmund cuts away the access steel to create the blade thickness of 1/5" (5 mm). "Note the constant flood of cutting oil in this stage of the milling process".

4 This is the steel bar after all the "machining" stages. The blade thickness is set; the handle tang cut and tapered; the "radius" cut on each end of the guard; the knife pattern traced onto the bar.

5 The model pattern of the knife after all sawing and rough outline grinding.

6 The final shape of the knife after the long process of grinding, filing and hand sanding and after Jere Davidson has just completed his masterful engraving. Now the all-steel piece is ready for its 2,400 mile trip to El Cajon (California) for heat treating by Paul Bos.

2

3

4

5

6

Opposite:

"Max's Fancy Hunter", 2004

Made of BG-42 steel, this Integral was heat treated by Paul Bos to 61 Rc. The handle material is stabilized California buckeye. Engraving by Jere Davidson.

Overall length 8 1/2" (216 mm).

Above, from the left:

"Loveless Design Drop hunter", 2002
Made of CPM 420 V steel, this Integral was heat treated by Paul Bos and hardened to 61 Rc. Engraving by Jere Davidson. The handle is ivory.
Overall length 8 1/4" (210 mm).

"Boot/Hunter", 1996
This 10th Anniversary Integral, one of ten made, is constructed from a single bar of 440C steel. Heat treated by Paul Bos to 58 Rc., it was engraved by Jere Davidson. The handle is ivory.
Overall length 9" (228 mm).

Opposite, from top left:

"Fillet Knife", 1998
This tapered-tang Fillet Model knife, heat treated by Paul Bos to 58 Rc, is made of 440C steel. Jere Davidson did the engraving and Linda Karst Stone covered the ivory handle with a beautiful nature study scrimshaw. Overall length 11 1/2" (292 mm).

"Loveless Design Straight Hunter", 1998
Made of BG-42 steel, this Integral was heat treated by Paul Bos to 61 Rc. The handle material is Desert Ironwood.
Overall length 8 1/2" (216 mm).

"Robin Cordle Hunter", 1999
Made of A-2 steel, this Integral with a Thuyia burl handle was heat treated by Paul Bos to 58 Rc.
Overall length 11 3/8" (289 mm).

"Western Skinner", 2004
Made of BG-42 steel and heat treated by Paul Bos to 61 Rc., this Integral has stabilized Curly Maple slabs for handle.
Overall length, 9 1/8" (231 mm).

"Loveless Design Nessmuk Skinner", 2004
Made of BG-42 steel and heat treated by Paul Bos to 61 Rc., this Integral has stabilized Black Ash burl slabs for handle.
Overall length, 8 1/4" (210 mm).

"Max's Large Crooked Skinner", 2003
Made of BG-42 steel and heat treated by Paul Bos to 61 Rc., this Integral has an ivory handle scrimshawed by Linda Karst Stone.
Overall length 8 7/8" (225 mm).

Above, from the left:

"American Push-Dagger", 1999

"This is my 2000th knife since I began making them in 1986".
An Integral push-dagger made of A-2 steel, heat treated to 58 Rc. by
Paul Bos. Scrimshaw on the ivory handle is by Linda Karst Stone and
the engraving is by Jere Davidson.
Overall length 8 3/8" (213 mm).

"Modern Bowie", 2000

Made of A-2 steel, this large Integral with a mastodon ivory handle
was heat treated by Paul Bos to 58 Rc. Jere Davidson did the
engraving.
Overall length 15 3/4" (400 mm).

Opposite, from the left:

"Max's Crooked Skinner", 2002

Made of BG-42 steel and heat
treated by Paul Bos to 61 Rc., this
Integral has Amboyna burl slabs for
handle. Engraved by Jere Davidson.
Overall length 8 1/4" (210 mm).

"Von Karls Death Star", 2004

Starting out in 1999 with a bar of
440C steel 1" (25 mm) thick and 2
1/2" (63 mm) wide, Edmund accepted
his most difficult project so far,
taking him five years to complete.
Heat treated by Paul Bos to 58 Rc.
and engraved by Jere Davidson,
this massive Integral has Desert
Ironwood handles.
Overall length 12 3/8" (314 mm).

"Max's Special Skinner", 1999

Made from a single bar of 440C steel,
this beautifully embellished Integral
was engraved by Jere Davidson and
inlaid with half an ounce of 24k gold.
Heat treated by Paul Bos to 58 Rc.
The handle is Cape Buffalo horn.
Overall length 8 1/2" (216 mm).

Jose C. de Braga
Quebec, Canada

Born in 1951, in the Azores Islands, Jose immigrated with his parents to Quebec, Canada, at the age of 3. His first contact with a knife was at the age of 5, when

his dad took him to the barber shop and the barber's daughter showed him a switchblade knife. The knife itself, as well as the idea that one could carry around such a useful tool with an interesting mechanism, was to him totally fascinating. He was hooked for the rest of his life. Being a 5-year-old with such an interest was quite frustrating, since no one would allow him to use or even get close to any kind of cutting device. So young Jose just started drawing them and became quite good at it. At the age of 10, when he finally received a small folding knife, he discovered that he could now carve three dimensional objects instead of just drawing them.

At 16, he still loved drawing new concepts, mechanisms and carving, but it was no longer "the real thing". Jose began to repair knives with a few tools in hand but found it difficult as he had too many other obligations. At 18 he joined the Canadian army for two years but left for ideological reasons. Another 15 years went by, owning and running a leather craft store, teaching leather crafts, promoting and marketing for an organization, working in the sales departments of various companies, getting involved with jewelry, wax carving, and teaching the latter to jewelers. Eventually, in October 1980, he met and later married Nicole, to whom Jose credits his becoming an artist knifemaker. Understanding his hidden passion, she encouraged him to do what he loves most.

Jose's work has been featured on magazine covers and in many articles. He won the 1989 and 1990 Most Unique Design awards and the 1992 Best Fantasy Knife at the Blade Show. He made swords for the "Highlander 3" movie and creates many one-of-a-kind custom art pieces to order.

Today Jose is the director of the Quebec Art Knife Makers Guild, founded by himself and two other Canadian knifemakers.

ART

Some years ago, my son, back home from the kindergarten, showed me a painting he had done that clearly conveyed his feeling of "enjoyment". When asked how his day was, he said: "Ho! Dad, we had so much fun. We had to paint with just our hands, so we plunged them into a bowl of paint and slapped them on a sheet of paper. There was paint everywhere. Everybody was laughing". It sure was a fine piece of art, for it did communicate the right feeling! If a 4-year-old kid can do it, anyone can. Life is a beautiful game with infinite opportunities to create. It's the greatest joy there is! So you see, you have no excuses not to ... Go ahead and create!

Opposite:
"Sirius Knight", 2004
Sirius is the brightest star in the collar of the Canis Major "The Dog" constellation, located in the Northern Hemisphere sky. The Sirius Knight is a short sword with a CPM S30V steel blade. The handle is made of 14k gold dust mixed with jet-stone composite set on a textured black paper-micarta base. *Habaki, tsuba, fushi* and *kashira* were carved from solid pieces of silicon-bronze. *Seppas*, front and rear appliqués, are made of Sterling silver. The Canis Major constellation is depicted on a 14k gold dust and jet-stone composite cabochon on the pommel of the *tsuka*, made of silver pins and a star engraved on a tiny 14k gold disk indicating Sirius.
Overall length 30 1/4" (768 mm).

CANIS MAJOR

SIRIUS

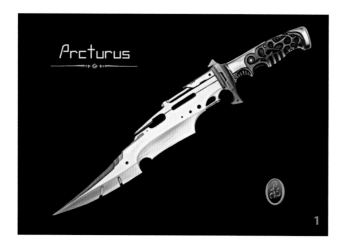

Arcturus

1

On the left:

The Making of "Arcturus"

"In a custom order the following steps are often skipped since the customer has his own idea on the subject. So the best you can do is to fulfill his dream to the utmost of your ability. But, on a self generated project, you will have a more successful impact if you can get the viewer involved in your effort. If your art tells the whole story, in spite of an extensive display of technical perfection, one will have no choice other than just admire it. Involving the viewer to start creating his own story when looking at one of my knives is difficult, since the object is in itself a complete story. Nevertheless, design, embellishments, details and shapes will get part of the job done. I will often dub my creations with fantasy, the name of a bright star or a constellation. And that usually does the job! The gears of imagination get cranked up and the viewer starts creating his own story..."

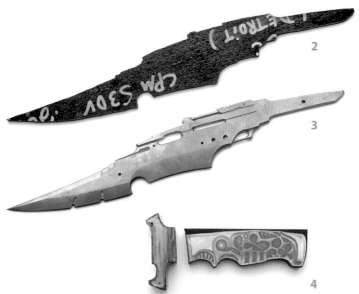

2

3

4

1 Jose starts by drawing the basic idea, slowly refining it to obtain a usable rendering. With today's computer technologies this has become a faster process, so he sometimes even adds color.

2 Once the blade blank is profiled, it is time to take it to the grinder, use files, pierce and sand it down to the desired design.

3 This is what the blade looks like after heat treatment.

4 The handle parts, guard, appliqués, etc. are rough-cut on solid pieces of silicon-bronze.

5 Last step is the fitting of all these parts to a perfect fit. Then the final carving and embellishing steps take place, giving birth to what was once only an idea on a computer-generated picture.

5

Opposite:

"Arcturus" 2004

Arcturus is the brightest star in the constellation of Bootes "The Herdsman". This knife has a 10" (254 mm) blade made of CPM S30V steel. The handle was carved from a jet stone composite and set on each side with a 4 mm hematite cabochon. The guard, blade sleeve and butt cap were carved from a solid piece of silicon-bronze. Spacers, appliqué and oval butt plate are of Sterling silver. On the butt-plate a 2 pt diamond marks Arcturus' position in the Bootes constellation.
Overall length 15 1/4" (387 mm).

ARCTURUS

BOÖTES

Above, from the left:

"Spica", 2004

Spica is the brightest star in the Virgo constellation and can be seen in skies of the Northern Hemisphere during the months of May and June. This dagger has a 5 1/4" (133 mm) blade, made of ATS-34 steel with a carved silicon-bronze sleeve. The guard plate is Sterling silver. The handle is carved pink ivory. A dark blue 10mm round sodalite cabochon is set in the pommel.
Overall length 9 1/4" (235 mm).

"Lyra", 2004

Lyra is a constellation located in Southern Hemisphere. This dagger has a 5" (127 mm), gun-blued Starrett-01 blade. Blade sleeve and guard plate are carved in silicon-bronze. The handle is carved Curly Maple and has a 6 mm x 8 mm oval onyx set in the pommel.
Overall length 9" (228 mm).

Opposite, from the top:

"Alcyone", 2004

One of the seven bright stars in the Pleiades, a group of stars found in the Taurus constellation. Alcyone was named after one of seven sisters and the daughter of Atlas and Pleione. In antiquity she was called upon by Greeks for protection against the elements of nature and evil.
The handle was made from the tip of a walrus tusk, with 3/8" (10 mm) sodalite cabochons set on each side. 14k gold particles are mixed into the lapis lazuli composite on the front section and pommel, where a 4 mm round cabochon garnet is inserted on Sterling silver. Guard and blade sleeve are carved out of a solid piece of silicon-bronze. Spacers are made of sheet Sterling silver.
Overall length 9 1/2" (241 mm) with a 5 1/2" (140 mm) stainless Damascus steel blade.

"Fomalhaut", 2004

Fomalhaut (pronounced foh-mah-low) is the eighteenth brightest star in the sky. It is located at the mouth of the Southern Fish, *Piscis Austrinus* (also known as *Piscis Australes*). In Persian history, Fomalhaut was equated with the god Zal; it is said to bestow charisma and to engender the test of remaining true to our ideals. The handle is carved out of lace wood. The 4 1/2" (114 mm) blade is made of ATS-34 steel. Blade sleeve and guard were carved out of a solid piece of silicon-bronze. Spacers are Sterling silver, and 3/8" (10 mm) onyx cabochons are set on each side of handle.
Overall length 8 1/4" (210 mm).

PLEIADES

ALCYONE

FOMALHAUT

PISCIS AUSTRINUS

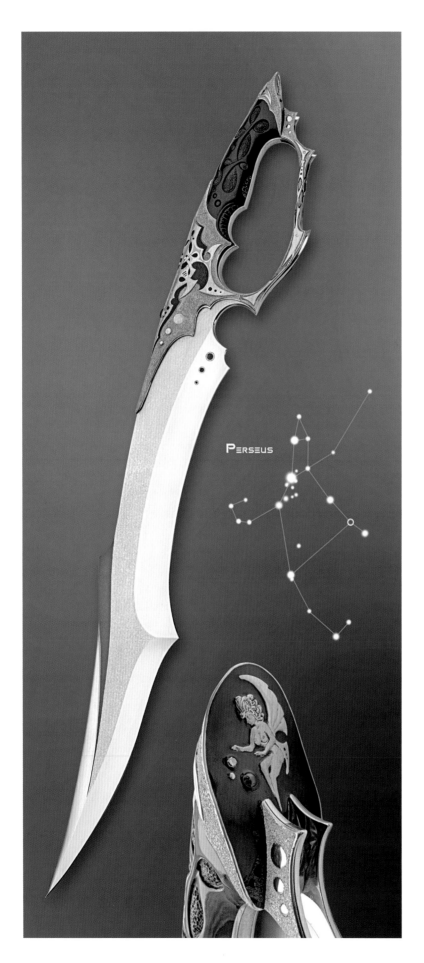

PERSEUS

On the left:
"Perseus", 2004
Named after the hero who cut off Medusa's head, giving birth to Pegasus from her blood, Perseus is found in Northern Hemisphere. Persus is a "D" guard short glaive, with a 15" (381 mm) CPM S30V steel blade. The handle is jet-stone composite with 14k gold, with oxidized Sterling silver appliqués set with two large oval red garnets. On the pommel face, along with a 4 pt diamond, 14k gold pin and an 8 mm red garnet, is the 14k gold carving of the figure of Medusa.
Overall length 23" (584 mm).

opposite:
"The Elder", 2004
The Elder's handle is made of stabilized Thuyia burl, with Sterling silver appliqués and a cloisonné of composite lapis lazuli containing embedded 14k gold particles.
The 7 1/2" (190 mm) blade is made of CPM S30V. The blade sleeve and guard were carved from a pure nickel-silver bar .
The figure on the pommel and the spacers are Sterling silver. The ring was carved and engraved from a solid piece of silicon-bronze.
Overall length12 3/4" (324 mm).

Jim Ence
Utah, USA

Jim was born in 1941, in Richfield, Utah, where he has spent his entire life. He grew up as a very inquisitive boy, always trying his hand at making something out of metal or wood. He made his first knife at the age of 9 out of an old car spring, thus beginning his life of knifemaking. He finished his education, served 6 years with the Army National Guard, got married, had two children, and went to work as a mine mechanic in a coal mine 3 miles underground. Now and then he made a hunting knife for a few chosen people.

In 1976 his friend Buster Warenski talked him into making a serious piece and attending a knife show with him in Las Vegas. That knife, a Bowie with an ebony handle, took the Best Fixed-Blade Knife award and Jim was hooked. Selling several knives at the 1977 Knifemakers Guild Show gave him the confidence he needed to continue making knives.

In 1978 he made a big decision, quitting his high-paying job to become a full-time knifemaker. His first years were difficult, but he never gave up, realizing his life-long dream with the consent and encouragement of his family and friends. He loves trying new things, especially those most say cannot be done. He liked making exact replicas of Michael Price Bradford daggers and other California knives. He has also made several folding knives. Jim believes strongly in sole authorship, therefore everything is done by himself, from forging his own Damascus, to engraving, carving, gold work and creating his own designs. Jim also does carvings in wood, ivory and other natural materials, and would like to try working with bronze. He is a member of the Art Knife Invitational, an elite group of 25 knifemakers from around the world.

When doing one of your own designed knives, there are many problems to overcome, ideas to work out, planning each piece to fit where it should and losing much sleep over grinding the blade. But when the knife is finished and someone says, "That is the best and the prettiest knife you have ever made", it makes it all worthwhile; and when someone says, "I can pick one of your knives out of a hundred", you can give yourself a pat on the back and say, job well done.

Jim Ence

Opposite, from the top:
"Golden Fire", 2003
The knife has a 17" (432 mm) beryllium-gold blade, handle fittings and guard. The handle is made of fire agate with fire opals and white sapphires on the pommel, center ring, feral and guard. Handle and guard are deeply engraved.
Overall length 22" (558 mm).

"Gladiator", 2003
The 14" (355 mm) 440C steel blade is engraved with a floral, poppy design. The guard, center ring and pommel are blued, have gold inlay, and have large emeralds and white sapphires set in them. The pommel has a unique basket with peddles and gold inlay, and a very large emerald on top. The handle itself is deeply carved old-walrus ivory with a floral scene to match the blade.
Overall length 19" (483 mm).
From the collection of Dave Nittinger.

"Persian Dagger", 2003
The 6" (152 mm) 440C steel blade has gold inlay on top. The nickel-silver bolster is carved and set with 32 emeralds. Stylized handle is high quality green jade. Matching steel sheath.
Overall length 11 1/2" (292 mm).

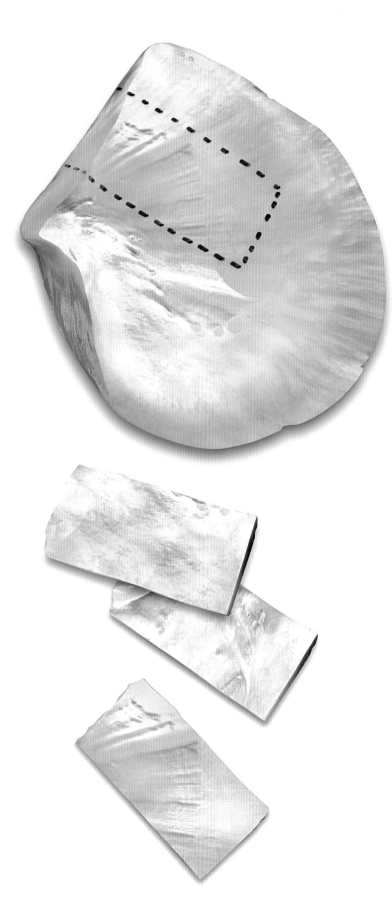

On the left:

Cutting Slabs of Mother-of-Pearl Shell

Mother-of-Pearl can be cut using a band saw and water to keep the dust down. Using a good mask is essential at all times. One goes as slowly as possible so as not to cause chipping. Mother-of-Pearl is actually quite a strong material and has been used to create jewelry for thousands of years.

Opposite:

"Mini Boot", 2004

This is the knife and sheath Jim Ence is known for. It is his knife. It has a 5 3/4" (146 mm) 440C stainless steel hollow-ground spear point blade, nickel-silver bolsters and floral engraving with a 24k gold button set with 7 large rubies. Premium white Mother-of-Pearl handle with a full 1" butt flair. The matching sheath is made of nickel-silver with a 24k gold frog button set with 7 large rubies. Overall length 11" (280 mm).

Contemporary "San Francisco" Daggers

On the left:

"Michael Price Bradford Bowie", 2003

Accurate replica of a Michael Price Bradford Bowie with an engraved miner scene on the 440C stainless steel blade. The handle is inlaid with gold quartz of different shades and from several sources, has 24k gold wire mosaic and is engraved on all sides and on the guard. Nickel-silver sheath with floral design inset with 24k gold.
Overall length 11" (280 mm).

Opposite, from the left:

"Bradford", 1999

A replica of the knife made in the 1850's by Michael Price for a chief of police in San Francisco, California. The 6 1/4" (158 mm) blade is made of 440C stainless steel. Wrapped handle with dark gold walrus ivory, 24k gold buttons and shield, engraved top to bottom and around bolster. Solid nickel-silver sheath with large oval of gold quartz and engraving.
Overall length 11" (280 mm).

"Bradford", 1999

Another replica of the knife made in the 1850's by Michael Price for a chief of police in San Francisco, California.
The 6 1/4" (158 mm) blade is made of 440C stainless steel. Wrapped handle with dark grey gold quartz mosaic design, 24k gold buttons and shield, engraved top to bottom and around bolster. Solid nickel-silver sheath with large oval of gold quartz and engraving.
Overall length 11" (280 mm).

"Bradford", 1995

Replica of a Bradford knife made by Michael Price. Ivory handle, 24k gold buttons and shield with extensive engraving and a 6 1/4" (158 mm) blade of 440C stainless steel.
The sheath is solid nickel-silver, covered with engraving from top to bottom.
Overall length 11" (280 mm).

"The Poppy Knife", 1996

A replica of The Poppy made by Michael Price in the 1850s. Handle is made from old walrus ivory, deeply carved with a poppy scene with buds and leaves, and 24k gold leaves on feral. 5 1/4" (133 mm) 440C stainless steel blade, nickel-silver sheath with a 24k gold poppy.
Overall length 10" (254 mm).

All four knives from the collection of Phil Lobred, USA.

On the left:

"Lion's Pride", 2004

An 11" (279 mm) 440C stainless steel, double hollow-ground blade, deeply carved and blued steel guard and ancient beach-washed walrus ivory handle. Jim did not change the shape of the ivory piece used for the handle, leaving it just the way it came out of the ocean. He deeply carved it with a pride of lions (small ones to a large male, with a pheasant sitting on its tail), adding 24k gold eyes and ending up with a three dimensional nature scene.

Overall length 17" (432 mm).

Opposite, from the top:

"Nine Hunters", 2004

The Bear, 4 3/4" (121 mm) 440C steel blade, stag handle, 24k gold carved bear, on the bolster, front and back.

Mom & Baby, 4 1/4" (108 mm) 440C steel blade, stag handle, 24k carved mom and baby raccoon, on the bolster, front and back.

The Big-Horn Sheep, 4 1/2" (114 mm) 440C steel blade, big-horn sheep handle, 24k gold carved big-horn sheep on the bolster.

The Leopard, 4 1/4" (108 mm) 440C steel blade, 24k gold carved leopard, jasper handle with a small band of gold beryllium with tracks, 24k gold leopard with tracks on the back.

The Wolf, 4 1/4" (108 mm) 440C steel blade, stag handle, 24k gold carved wolf, front and back.

The Snake, 3 1/2" (89 mm) 440C steel blade, stag handle, 24k gold carved snake and mongoose.

The Owl, 2 3/4" (70 mm) 440C steel blade, stag handle, 24k gold carved hoot owl.

The Elephant, 3" (76 mm) 440C steel blade, pearl handle, 24k gold carved elephant.

Raccoon, 3 1/4" (82 mm) 440C steel blade, stag handle, 24k gold carved raccoon, front and back.

Jerry Fisk
Arkansas, USA

Jerry Fisk was born in Eugene, Oregon, in 1953, but his family soon moved to Arkansas, where he has since resided. At the tender age of 10 he became fascinated with the art of knifemaking after visiting the reconstructed blacksmith shop of James Black in nearby Washington, Arkansas. Needless to say, it was Black who made the knife for the famous James Bowie, that soon became known as "the Bowie". As a youngster, Jerry began handcrafting blades by forging steel in a small coal-fired forge. Then, as he gained knowledge, he moved on to more modern equipment. In 1989 he became the 17th Mastersmith in the ABS. He was elected to the Board of Directors of the ABS in 1994, as well as serving as one of the Mastersmiths who review the work of applicants for the MS stamp. He also serves as the ABS liaison officer to the Texarkana College's Bill Moran School of Bladesmithing in Washington, Arkansas. At present, this is the world's only school of bladesmithing. Unlike many of his contemporaries, Fisk specializes in fixed-blade knives, the majority of which are fighter or Bowie designs. Some feature Damascus patterned blades, others "plain" steel forged blades. But whatever, they are all exceptional pieces of art. His beautiful knives have garnered him numerous awards over the years, and if you ask him which award he values most, don't be surprised when he tells you it was being the first bladesmith to receive the Governor's Folk Life and Traditional Arts Award in 1997 from the Governor of Arkansas. He was also nominated to receive the coveted status of National Living Treasure. Prior to his being named, only three artisans had been awarded this status.

As might be expected, Fisk knives are owned and cherished by collectors/investors around the world. They might be outdoorsman or European royalty, but whoever, they respect Jerry's skills as a bladesmith, and love the clean lines present in all of his knives. His creations are something a true collector aspires to attain.

I make knives and edged tools. I do this because of a life-long interest and desire. The only limits to this field are what I put on myself, at times blending both centuries-old techniques and modern methods. Forging knives for a living has for centuries been a hot and dirty job. It is no different now. The glamor fades quickly as you burn the shirts off your body. I prefer designs drawn from something simulating nature and prefer to work with natural materials.

When someone asked me why I made knives, I said "To show that I lived". I know my work will last hundreds of years longer than I will, so now they will know.

Jerry L Fisk

Opposite:
"Ants", 2001
Jerry's Damascus blade Camp Knives have a tremendous appeal. This knife has a complicated Damascus pattern that was forged into a "W" pattern then had a traditional Ladder pattern forged into that pattern. The mountings are 24k gold over silver. The handle is a fossilized artifact war club. It was found in the ground with its tip broken off, possibly during use. Jerry kept the back-slot as it was originally made, to fit an oosic bone. He tried to keep it as authentic as possible, with a little saw work to touch up its shape. Ants and spiders were carved on the handle so that they appear to be still crawling on it, in the ground. The ants and spiders were then covered in gold foil to match the mountings.
Overall length 16" (406 mm).

On the left:

Forging Steel

1 The bridge anvil and the roll-around tool cart that holds all the forge tools Jerry need for a particular forging project.
2 Forge welding a billet of Damascus on the air hammer. The air hammer gives much better control compared to mechanical hammers.
3 Hand welding a billet of Damascus.
4 Wire brushing the scale from a billet, to check the welds.

Opposite:

"Sendero" Hunter, 2004

"This Sendero Hunter is unique in that it is the only time I have put this particular handle design on a regular Sendero design. This handle normally goes on the Integral Sendero. The handle material on this particular Sendero is sambar stag. The Damascus blade has a Raindrop pattern, signifying "into each life some rain must fall". The stainless steel guard is engraved with a chain design, reminding us all that each of us is also bound by our own chains in some form or another".
Overall length 9" (228 mm).

On the left:

Two "Sendro" Hunters, 2002

This is the design for which Jerry Fisk is most recognizable. Both of the knives shown are forged of carbon steel. The stag handled knife (shown on the right) is the Bird and Trout version of the Sendero. It also has the traditional good luck Wheat pattern engraved onto the stainless steel guard. The handle material on the other Sendero shown here is a piece of fossilized Stellar Sea Cow bone. These marine mammals became extinct after the natives discovered that they tasted like chicken. The stainless steel guard and pins are engraved with beading. This is achieved by raising thousands of small beads, one at a time, using a hand-held tool. The escutcheon inlaid into the handle is engraved with scroll work. One of the most frequent comments upon seeing the Sendero design is *"Ooh, I want one of those".*
Overall length 8 1/2" (216 mm).

Opposite:

"Hope's Unicorn" Mediterranean Dirks, 2002

The Mediterranean Dirk is probably the world's most-copied and most influential knife, design-wise. Largely unchanged from the Middle Ages, it was also the forerunner of the American Bowie Knife. These knives work well in the kitchen or out in the field.

"My favorite personal knife, which I made for myself, was an integral Dirk. Integrals are rapidly becoming popular again in the USA. When I forge one from Damascus, first I weld the billet, forge it round, forge the blade and at the end forge in the pattern. The Damascus blade shown here has a Raindrop pattern forged in. Both handles are made of unicorn horn. You must be pure of heart to see a unicorn. I see them all the time, then run out and cut their horns off... Well, it's really made of antique elephant ivory carved in an old style; gain twist fluting that represents a unicorn horn".

The Integral Damascus blade (shown on the left) has carving on the pommel. The carbon steel blade (on the right) has the first engraving Jerry put on a blade. Both knives have 24k gold pommels.
Overall lengths of each 14 1/2" (368 mm).

Above, from the left:

"Sendero Bowie", 2003

"I have made the Southern Bowie as long as I have made knives, with very few changes in the design. This is a very popular design for people that like the American Bowie as it is very traditional in its design". The Sendero Bowie shown here is a Raindrop pattern Damascus blade. The stainless steel guard, ferrule and pommel are engraved with leaves. The handle materials are of fossil mammoth ivory. Overall length 15" (381 mm).

"The Gumbyahha", 2003

This is a boot knife that has a sharpened clip. The handle material for this knife is mammoth ivory from the same tusk Sendero Bowie seen here. The pattern in the Damascus blade of the boot knife is the traditional Viking Wolf-Tooth pattern. The guard and pins are stainless steel and engraved to match the Bowie. *"Having a matching set is an outstanding addition to anyone's collection".* Overall length 8 1/2" (216 mm).

"Sendro", 2002

The third knife shown with close-up view on the far left, is another look at Jerry's Sendro model. The handle is Sambar stag and the stainless steel guard has a traditional Wheat pattern engraved for good luck. The pins are engraved with flowers. The blade has a Wolf-Tooth Damascus pattern. *"This knife looks good wherever you find yourself, be it just looking at your collection or using it in the field".* Overall length 8 3/4" (222 mm).

Opposite, from the left:

"Southwest Bowie", 2002

The Southern Bowie has a handle of sheep horn, a natural material that has outstanding characteristics for knife handle material. This particular Bowie has a Raindrop pattern Damascus, forged in, and a blued-steel guard and ferrule. *"This is a plain looking knife until you hold it. Then you just gotta go cut something".* Overall length 15 1/2" (394 mm).

"Southwest Bowie", 2003

This knife has has an antique ivory handle. *"Ivory is one of the true classic handle materials and always helps hold the value of a knife, with this particular antique ivory being a fossilized walrus tusk".* The S-shaped guard on this knife was forged then carved with sea shells on the ends. The wide ferrule is carved and the materials for both guard and ferrule are 24k gold over silver. The Damascus blade is a combination of Raindrop and Wolf-Tooth pattern forged in. Overall length 15 1/2" (394 mm).

Larry Fuegen
Arizona, USA

Born in 1952, Larry has been making things since he was a child growing up on his parents' cattle ranch in Reliance, South Dakota. An early fascination with knives compelled him to take apart old knives then apply new handles and reshape the blades. He made his first knife in 1963.

He started forging blades in 1975 and became a full-time bladesmith in 1987. In 1989 he received his Master Smith rating from the American Bladesmith Society. Larry is also a member of the Art Knife Invitational group, representing 25 of the top makers, with each member being voted in by the other makers. Their show every two years in San Diego, California, is a must-see for all serious knife collectors.

Larry performs all of the work on each of his knives and sheaths; he does not job out any step in the knifemaking process or use any ready-made parts. A unique feature of every fixed-blade knife that leaves his shop is the high-quality hand-sewn leather sheath, which is designed to complement the finished knife.

Larry uses very few power tools; relying on many small-hand held tools to create his Art Knives. His desire to be the sole author of his work allows him to offer truly unique hand-made creations. The art folder "Alaric King of the Visigoths", which is the only knife in the permanent collection of the Renwick Gallery of the National Museum of American Art, the Smithsonian Institution, is a fine example of Larry's dedication to the Art Knife concept.

His classic style and use of colors, textures and shapes continues to evolve as he masters a wider range of materials and techniques. Developing a new idea and then taking it in different directions to see what new possibilities it offers is the challenge Larry enjoys most. With the help of his wife, Linda, who takes care of the office duties, Larry looks forward to working with his collectors on new and exciting projects.

Creating hand-forged custom knives has been my passion for the past thirty years and a full-time profession since 1987. To forge a blade, the smith puts his soul into the blade through his hard work, experience and determination. It isn't the easiest or fastest way to make a blade, but I find the challenge very rewarding, and the end result is well worth the extra effort.

The challenge of creating art knives continues to grow and evolve as new materials and ideas are tried. It is this challenge and a constant desire to create that makes this profession so exciting and rewarding to me as an artist and craftsman.

Opposite:
"Unicorn Dagger", 2003
This dagger was inspired by the 15th-century "Unicorn Sword" of Charles the Bold, Duke of Burgundy. For several hundred years, the Vikings sold narwhal ivory to the Europeans, who believed it was the magical horn of the fabled unicorn. To the Europeans, the unicorn represented many things that they themselves tried to achieve, including power, loyalty and virtue. A ruby, pearls, and engraved designs were used on the original sword and were symbols associated with the Order of the Golden Fleece, a medieval order of knights. The hand-forged 9 1/2" (241 mm) blade is made of 1095 carbon steel. The handle is narwhal ivory.
Overall length, 16" (406 mm).
From the collection of Don Guild, Hawaii.

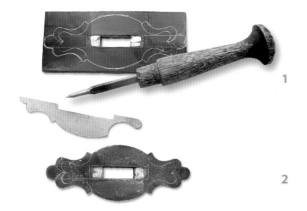

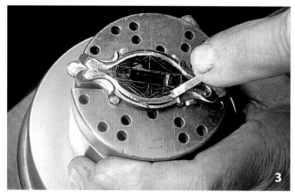

The Steel Guard and Carved Handle

"It has always been my desire to be the sole author of each of my knives. To accomplish this over the years I've learned to forge, heat treat, work with different materials, carve, engrave, gold and silversmith, and do leather work. I've also developed my own unique style of file work. By combining the various materials, types of embellishments and construction techniques, there are endless ways to create one-of-a-kind Art Knives".

1 A rectangular slot for the tang is cut with a jewelers saw, for the blade to pass through, and then carefully hand-filed to get a precise fit. The outline of the guard is scribed onto the surface using a brass template designed especially for this knife.

2 Excess material is carefully cut, ground and filed away to create this profiled guard blank.

3 The background is carved away with a flat graver to provide depth and contrast.

4 As the work progresses on the guard, the outside edges are beveled with files and sanded to a 600 grit finish. The process of carving the background and beveling the edges alternates back and forth until the final shape is even and balanced on all surfaces on the front and the back of the guard.

5 The transformation of a flat piece of steel into the carved, textured and polished guard is complete. Before final assembly, the guard will be given an antiqued brown finish. This will address the three important parts needed to create an Art Knife - shape, texture and color.

6 After the basic design is carved into the Desert Ironwood handle, all of the carved surfaces are finished by handsanding using small sanding sticks and strips of emery cloth.

Opposite:

"Gentleman's Bowie", 2004

This Bowie incorporates many of the features of the classic Bowie knife of the late 1800s. The 8" (203 mm) hand-forged carbon steel blade is hand-sanded to a 1200 grit satin finish. A carved steel guard and fileworked handle frame are rust browned to create a subtle color combination with the handle, and a strong visual connection with the blade. The hand-carved Desert Ironwood handle features smooth and textured surfaces in a fleur-de-lis design. An engraved nickel-silver band and fileworked liners complete the handle. A custom tooled leather sheath with an exotic ostrich leg overlay, accompany the Bowie. Overall length is 12 1/2" (318 mm).

On the left:

Carved Damascus Fighters, 1996

"The tangs and liners on both of these fighters exhibit my unique style of file work. Although both knives use the same basic materials, the combination of colors, textures, size and shape demonstrates the wide range of possibilities these materials offer".

On the left, a **Small Damascus Fighter** with a 2 1/2 " (63 mm) Zigzag Damascus blade and a carved fossil walrus ivory handle. Fittings are carved, textured and polished steel with 14k gold pins.

Overall length 6 1/2" (165 mm).

On the right, a **Large Fighter** with a 7 1/2" (190 mm) Starburst Damascus blade and a carved fossil walrus ivory handle. Fittings are carved, textured and polished steel with 14k gold pins.

Overall length 13 1/2" (343 mm).

Both knives from the collection of Brian Leyden, USA.

Opposite, from the top:

"Black Buffalo Horn Push-Dagger", 1992

The blade is San Mai Damascus using wrought iron steel with a 1095 carbon steel core. The handle is carved black buffalo horn.

Overall length 5 1/2" (140 mm).

"Carved Pearl Push-Dagger", 1995

Deeply carved Mother-of-Pearl handle with 14k gold accent.

Overall length 5 1/2" (140 mm).

Both of these push-daggers feature full file work on the tangs and liners.

"The concept for these push-daggers evolved from an idea for a small single-edged knife that was easy to carry, secure in the hand and visually exciting. They became small pieces of sculpture to be carried, used and admired".

Both knives from the collection of Brian Leyden, USA.

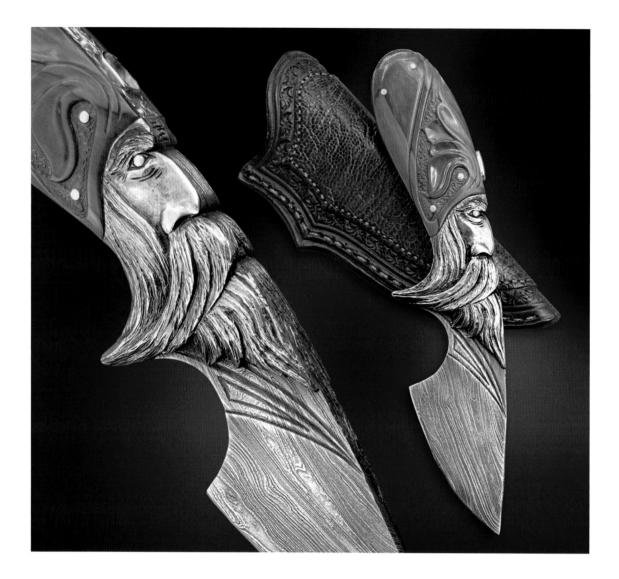

Above:

"Personal Carry Art knife", 2003

The 3" (76 mm) blade is made of Linear pattern Damascus. The bolsters are carved steel. The handle is carved mammoth ivory with 14k gold pins and bezel with Black-Lip Pearl cabochon. The tang and liners feature full file work. The custom sheath has a tooled border with an ostrich leg overlay. Overall length 6 1/2" (165 mm).

"This small knife revolves around the bolster, which is carved to resemble the face of an old man with his large mustache and beard. He wears a large hat with carved designs. Is he a high priest, or the leader of an ancient civilization? The Linear Damascus blade with its carved design represents his tailored garment of wondrously exotic material".

Opposite, from the top:

"Carved Art Dagger", 2001

The carved Zigzag Damascus steel blade, carved mammoth ivory handle with 14k gold bands and carved French grayed steel guard are complemented by a beautiful scabbard of black calfskin with French grayed steel fittings and 14k gold trimmings. Overall length 14" (356 mm).

Matching "Dagger and Bowie", 1999 and 2002

Both knives have carved Mother-of-Pearl handles and carved rust blued steel guards and bolsters with 14k gold bands.

Overall lengths: The dagger is 13" (330 mm) and the Bowie is 15 1/2" (394 mm).

"This trio of knives showcases the beauty of the deeply carved materials. By carving the ivory and mother of pearl handles, the inner beauty of the materials is brought to the surface. The grain of the ivory is exposed and the luster and iridescence of the pearl becomes more eye-catching. I also feel that carving creates shadows, and as the knife is rotated, new surfaces are exposed to the light".

Chantal Gilbert
Quebec, Canada

Born in Quebec City in 1958, Chantal Gilbert grew up in a family of 15 children. Chantal is first and foremost a jeweler and earned widespread recognition as such in the 1980s.

Jewelry has long been a passionate means of expression for her. Through her craft she has become familiar with gold and silver, two precious metals with which she has developed a lasting relationship.

Toward the end of the 1980s, the decorative aspect of her work gave way to a more sculptural trend, and in 1991 she turned her interest to a purely functional tool, the knife, taking up knifemaking and creating her own Damascus steel. Over the last few years, Chantal Gilbert's art has shifted from decorative objects to those that tell a story while maintaining their shape and utilitarian aspect. Her knives have fascinating tales to tell, yet they remain unequivocally what they were meant to be: sharp, timeless, ergonomic and at the same time functional, accessible and understandable.

What truly interests Chantal is the unspoken. Through various portrayals of the knife, she bears witness to its psychological impact and the true role this indispensable tool plays in the development of the real and imaginary world. Part of her work stems from a desire to codify the knife in a different way. Her collection of creatures, for instance, takes on an allegorical sense. The pieces are no longer weapons or tools, and her unique appropriation of the knife results in stunning works of art rather than merely utilitarian objects. This approach reflects a twofold desire: to relate to the object in its most primary function and to move away from traditional knifemaking toward a typically feminine lyricism.

Gilbert has been the recipient of many grants and honors for her jewelry and as a knifemaker. Her knives have found their way into collections in many countries around the world. They are on sale in galleries in France, Switzerland, Sweden and the United States. Since 1991, Chantal Gilbert has been teaching at the Quebec City Jewelry School.

I entered the world of knifemaking by way of jewelry. Now, years later, I am able to explore new areas of aesthetics with greater sensitivity. Viewing things in a new light, I want to bring out the essence of the "tool symbol". My mission testifies to my need to attach myself to the meanings in the object with a feminine lyricism not found in traditional knifemaking, which is essentially masculine.

Once the creative process has been completed and the work is finished, a multitude of interpretations suggest themselves. My accomplice is matter, into which I integrate my feelings. I act upon it through modulation, rhythm and formation of the idea, thus transposing my vision of the world.

Chantal Gilbert

Opposite, from the top:

"La Bestiole", 1997
Half insect, half bird, La Bestiol's 18k gold wings bear a green tourmaline stone of exceptional color. Its body and legs are of Sterling silver. The handle is Sterling silver, as is the stand. The blade/beak, is Damascus steel forged by the French smith Doursin. This small creature measures 5 11/16" (145 mm).

"Bécassine", 1997
The handle and the legs of Bécassine are of Sterling silver. "I wanted it to be dancing and full of joy. Its caricatured gait makes one momentarily forget the role of its ATS-34 steel blade". Overall length 5 14/16" (150 mm).

"Le Minotaure", 2000
A mythological creature with a human body and the head of a bull. "My Minotaure is a free interpretation of the Cretan myth. The only thing wild about the beast is the way it looks". The body is of Sterling silver and snakewood, the blade of Damascus steel. Overall length 6 11/16" (170 mm).

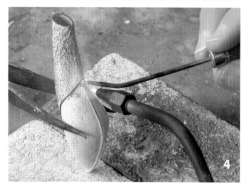

Creating The Handle

1 Shaping the handle. When making the handles for her knives, Chantal utilizes techniques from the world of Jewelry and goldsmithing. She shapes the different parts out of precious metals, using hammers and other tools employed in creating jewelry. The guard is molded in a wooden matrix, which allows the sides of the metal to close toward each other without provoking any alteration to their surfaces.

2 Assembling the back part of the handle. The handle for this knife is made of two parts, each shaped like a shell. A third "shell" previously soldered inside one of them creates an aperture within the body of the knife, for aesthetic and symbolic effect. Once the rough shaping of all the parts has been completed, Chantal uses different files and emery papers to bring the two parts of the knife to a high-quality finish before the final assembling.

3-4 Soldering. Now all the parts are soldered together, each covering the one inside it. This is the most delicate moment, demanding precise alignment and accurate soldering so as not to leave any smudge or blemish.

5 Stone setting and decorating. Chantal made the blade from Damascus steel forged by Nick Smolen, who creates some magnificent steels that complement the jewelry quality of her knife art. The decorative elements, made of 18k gold are now welded to the handle and the precious stone is ready to be set. The handle is oxidized to create many shades and contrasts that will bring out the different treatment and texturing of the metal serfaces. The final step will be the setting of the garnet and insertion of the pheasant's feather.

Opposite:
"My Precious", 2004
Silver, gold, Nick Smolen's Damascus steel, a garnet and a pheasant's feather were combined to create this knife sculpture. The feather can be removed at anytime, turning this piece of functional art into a knife. Overall length 6 1/2" (165 mm).

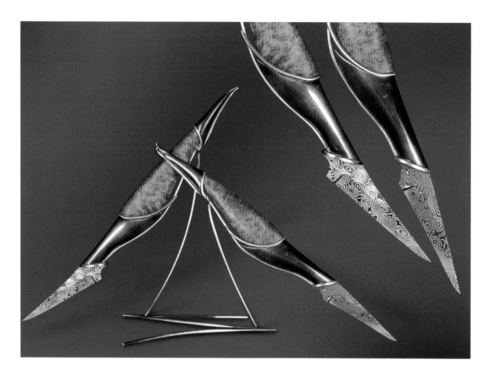

"La baleine", 1994

This piece is one of Chantal's first knife creations. Its handle was entirely fashioned and assembled from Sterling silver. The blade is of ATS-34 steel. It features a guilloched pattern along its entire length. Overall length 7 7/8" (200 mm).

"Calmar", 1997

"The creation of Calmar was an important moment in the development of my work with knives. It was the first time I used bronze along with silver and ebony. The knife's curved form, difficult to perceive in photos, is surprisingly ergonomic. I perforated the blade in a moment of daring creativity, knowing that purists might not appreciate the gesture. I am quite attached to this piece and only agreed to part with it because its current owner is a good friend". Sterling silver handle with bronze and ebony, Damascus blade. Overall length 7 7/8" (200 mm).

"Les 2 Petits Amours", 1995

"Two small knives that have no intent other than to please". Both are Sterling silver and 18k gold; however, one is set with a rhodolite stone, the other with lapis lazuli. Both blades are ATS-34 steel. Each knife measures 3 15/16" (100 mm).

"Un Air de Famille", 1998

"Three knives emerging from one root. The piece as a whole represents the connections that engender and unite people, from the umbilical cord to the roots that nourish both the family and society as a whole. The blades evoke the fragility of union, parting and renewal. Children will, of course, one day, leave the nest...".

The handles of these knives are Sterling silver, with different surface treatments, shapes, construction and assembly. The blades are Damascus steel forged by the French knifemaker Doursin. The entire sculpture measures 7 7/8" x 5 1/3" x 2/10" (200x135x5 mm).

Above:

"I always approach the concept of the knife as a reference to humanity. Several pieces in my current collection evoke the concept of duality, exploring the tensions generated when opposites meet. These issues of personal concern have resulted in indissociable duos, such as Les Deux Grâces, Les Grands Hérons and Basse-cour".

"Les Deux Grâces", 2002

"At first glance, the two knives that make up this pair would seem to be joined. However, the distinct characteristics of each are apparent. One is straight, drawn out and precise. The other is teasingly contorted but just as ergonomic. Rigidly and flexibly they interrogate and respond to one another". The knives are made of bronze, Sterling silver and Amboyna burl. The blade is Damascus steel forged by Nick Smolen. Overall length 9 1/2" (240 mm).

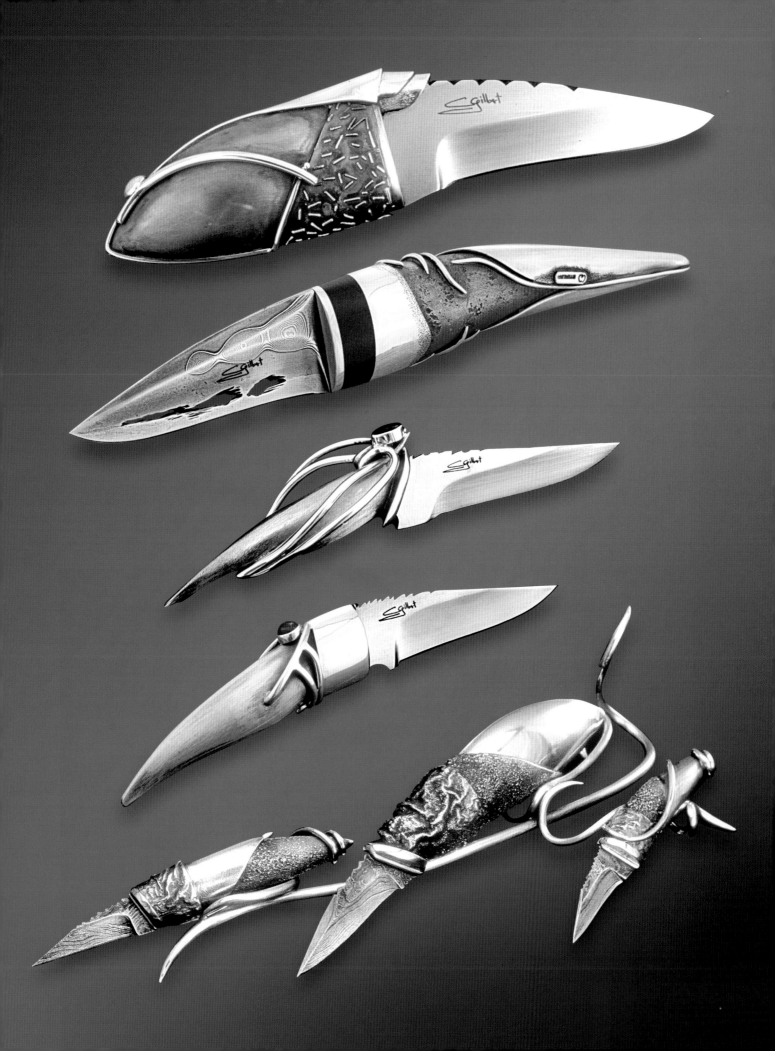

Above:

"Les Grands Hérons", 2001

"The idea of the pair is presented once again in this piece. While constituting a whole, these knives play each other individually. Interactive, they complement each other, repelling, attracting, facing, and seeking each other, as couples often do".

Both were created in Sterling silver and fossilized Mammoth ivory. Blades created from Damascus steel made by Nick Smolen. Overall lengths 11 2/5" and 11 4/5" (290 and 300 mm).

Opposite, from the top:

"Urbanoïde", 2001

"City mouse or country mouse? The bronze and Sterling silver body evokes alleyways and concrete paths, and its blade/beak that of a garbage picker. I created the blade of this playful rodent from Damascus steel forged by Nick Smolen".

Overall length 11 2/5" (290 mm).

"Gracile", 2000

"My interest in metalwork has always been guided by a single obsession, that of transforming metal, an inherently cold and lifeless substance, into something vibrant and alive. My desire to see metal in constant, figurative movement has inspired me to created insects and birds that walk, fly and run; they are, in fact, allegories of the weapon-tool. An experiment in poetically denaturalizing the knife, Gracile is my favorite insect knife: feminine, graceful and beautifully fragile on its tiny, delicate legs".

On its silver body, set in 18k gold, is a rhodolite stone. The hilt is mammoth ivory and the blade Damascus steel.

Overall length 9 4/5" (250 mm).

"Basse-cour", 2001

"What is interesting about the art knife is its dual relations to art and utility. As a commonplace object on the one hand and art object on the other, it cohabits the both terrains. The two knives that make up Basse-cour are among the most utilitarian of my collection, because this rooster and hen are in fact cheese knives".

The handles are Sterling silver and bronze and the hilt is snakewood. The blade is made of ATS-34 steel.

Overall lengths 6" (150 mm) and 7 7/8" (200 mm).

Tim Hancock
Arizona, USA

Tim was born in 1954 into a family of western heritage. Raised in Arizona in the cowboy culture and life style, Tim endeavored to learn all the necessary skills to become a top hand. In the late 70's, he fell in love with and married a fine woman named Susan and they had two wonderful daughters, Vanessa and Terrah. Tim's first career was as a pipe welder in the construction of nuclear power stations.

Tim's first "masterpiece" came into being in 1987 stemming from a challenge from his father. As the story goes, Tim was admiring a collection of Indian artifacts that his father had on display. One of the items was an original knife sheath. Tim said "That is a neat sheath. Too bad you don't have a knife to display in it." Dad said, "Well I guess any decent farrier should be able to make a knife." In his youth, Tim had learned the art of horse shoeing and forging from his father and immediately knew who he was referring to. The gauntlet had been thrown down! So it began; his Dad got that first knife.

Each and every knife became a challenge to do a better job. Tim's goals were simple: superior function first, followed by design and finally, artistic appeal. The challenge seems never to have ended for Tim and because of his efforts to meet each new challenge, he has become a well-known and respected knifemaker along the way.

While his mainstay is fixed-blade knives, especially Bowies, he does enjoy making folders as well. He has been recognized as a Master Bladesmith since 1994 and has received numerous awards in his career.

In 2001, Tim was inducted into the prestigious Art Knife Invitational (AKI) show. According to Tim, being recognized by some of the most respected knife makers of all time is one of the greatest highlights of his career.

Knifemaking is an art form that seemingly never ceases to present new concepts to learn and opportunities for personal expression. As if that's not enough, I have never met a better group of people from either side of the show table. To sum it up, this is a phenomenal experience for me. I strive to make each knife possess three components: functional integrity, quality craftsmanship and aesthetic appeal. Strong and decisive lines have always been important to my designs. Embellishment is secondary, but never omitted.
To those who have enthusiastically supported this art form with the same passion we makers bring to our work, I wish to convey my deepest feelings of appreciation.

Timothy J. Hancock

Opposite:
"California Dagger No. 1", 2001
"This is the first knife that I made in this wonderful style, and it was a very detailed metal-forming project to say the least". The blade is ATS-34, the handle parts are German silver and 18k gold, and the scales are mastodon ivory. The sheath is full German silver with a gold button. The exquisite engraving was done by master engraver Bryan Bridges. Overall length 11" (280 mm).

Making the Cowboy Bowie

1 The high carbon steel is stacked up to start the process of making the Damascus for the Featured Knife. The anvil seen in the picture was purchased new when Tim was 13 years old. Not the best anvil he owns but certainly one of the most sentimental.

2 Forge welding the billet of steel into one solid bar using an old #50 Little Giant mechanical power hammer.

3 Taking a look at the blade as it is forged into shape, planning the next step.

4 The parts of the knife: guard, spacer, handle frame, liners, pommel bolsters, pearl scales and the blade, all finished, etched and ready for final assembly.

Tim Hancock individually numbered his first 179 knives, and in 1995 he started using the year with his MS in the center. Non-forged blades have no MS mark, and all of his knives are marked with his surname. His knives gain a decisive level of recognition without seeing the maker's mark. This is something he had hoped to achieve in making his impression on the knife world. As a full-time maker Tim produces between 25 and 50 knives each year.

Opposite:

"Cowboy Bowie", 2004, with matching folder.

"This design has also been very well received by the collectors". It is an all-Damascus knife. The blade is Ladder pattern Damascus with a sweeping clip. The guard, pommel and handle frame are also Ladder pattern steel. The spacer is Twist pattern Damascus that has been boarder cut and grooved. The pommel has the same cuts and groove as well. The scales are of genuine Mother-of-Pearl shell mounted over German silver liners that are file worked in a combination of Tim's "XO" pattern and notching. The sheath is leather with sharkskin overlay, boarder tooling, and a German silver frog post button. Overall length 11 1/4" (286 mm). This particular knife was made to create a matching pair for Tim's pearl lockback folder made for the 2001 AKI show.

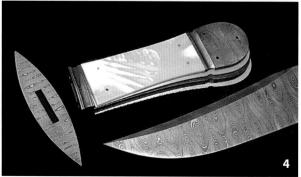

Above:

"Mastodon Hunter", 2003

"This was a fantastic piece of mastodon ivory, around which I built this knife".

The Ladder pattern Damascus blade sports a long straight clip and a Spanish notch. The tear-shaped guard, boarder cut and grooved spacer and handle frame are all Twist pattern Damascus. The liners are German silver file worked all around with notch and half-vine pattern. The leather sheath has sharkskin overlay. Overall length 9" (228 mm).

Opposite, from the top:

"Tejas Bowie", 2003

This mid-sized gent's Bowie has a Ladder pattern Damascus blade with a sweeping clip and a Spanish notch. The "S" style scroll guard is forged of Twist pattern Damascus, the boarder cut spacer and similar butt cap are connected with a treaded finial of Damascus as well. The fittings are highlighted with spacers of German silver. The ebony handle is cross-grooved and adorned with domed German silver pins. The sheath is formed leather with German silver tip and throat with Damascus trim. Overall length 12 1/2" (318 mm).

"Hancock Bowie", 2003

"This is my conception of an excellent fighting knife design. The blade is multi-faceted, similar to that of a Japanese sword".

The blade and fittings are Damascus, the spacers, file worked liners, and tang wrap are German silver. The scales are of colored mastodon ivory. This knife won "Best Fighter" and "Best of Show" at the 2003 Arizona Knife Collectors Show. Overall length 15" (381 mm).

On the left:
"Will and Finck", 2000
Styled like those of the 1800s. The hand-forged blade is of 52100 high carbon steel. The guard and adorning domed pins are German silver mounted onto a perfect piece of elephant ivory. The sheath is full German silver with a spring loaded mechanical belt clip. Winner of "Best Fixed Blade" at the 2000 Blade Show in Atlanta. Overall length 11" (280 mm).

Opposite, from the top:
"Straight-Back Dog Bone", 2001
"The Dog Bone Bowie has been one of my favorite styles of all time. This one is Damascus all the way, the blade, fittings, handle frame, finial and escutcheon plates. I used spacers and liners of German silver for highlights and handle scales of creamy walrus ivory, which is multi-faceted for that fantastic feel". The domed buttons hold the handle together with peened pins. The sheath is formed leather with German silver tip and throat and Damascus button and point.
Overall length 15" (381 mm)
"Clip-Point Dog Bone", 2001
This "Dog Bone" is made with Damascus, lots of file work and colored walrus ivory. The tang and pommel are wrapped in the tradition of the originals of the 1800s. The sheath is formed of German silver to closely fit the blade and is mounted with Damascus trim.
Overall length 15" (381mm).
"Studded Dagger", 2001
This dagger sports Tim Hancock's high-contrast Damascus a sculpted guard, five-piece spacer, a three-piece finial and clean walrus ivory decorated with a myriad of domed German silver pins. The sheath is formed leather with German silver tip and throat with Damascus trim. Winner of "Best Damascus" at Blade Show West 2001. Overall length 12" (305 mm).

Gil Hibben
Kentucky, USA

Gilbert W. Hibben was born in Wyoming, in 1935. In his own quiet and unassuming way, Hibben has made his mark in the world of handmade knives. But, while many only know of him as a knifemaker and designer, another side of him is that he has performed with many singing and musical groups over the years, including the world-famous Mormon Tabernacle Choir. He has also helped win two world championships in Barbershop Chorus competitions with the Louisville Thorougbred Chorus. In a totally different field, he holds a black belt in judo as well as a 6th-degree black belt in Kenpo karate.

Gil made his first knife as a youngster in 1950, a big Bowie, simply because he couldn't afford to buy one. He labored at least 60 hours using a stone grinder, files and a hand drill to make that knife, which like many others, he gave away to family and friends. Upon his discharge from the navy in 1956, Gil settled in Salt Lake City and soon began making more knives in his spare time. When he sold a Bowie for $45, he was hooked, finding it hard to believe people would pay for knives. Knifemaking was consuming more of his time now, so he quit his "real job" and went full-time in 1964. A year later one of his knives was featured on the cover of Guns & Ammo magazine, and this "local" maker was now recognized nationally. During the following five years he had the pleasure of working with and teaching a number of young men who would also go on to become "names" in the world of custom knives. He is now settled with his wife, Linda, in LaGrange, Kentucky, where he's still very active.

Recognizing the fact that he has been very successful in his career as a knifemaker and designer, Gil says, *"We all have inner guidance and I would like to give credit to that. It's been like following a dream".* He has, indeed, built has life around knives, an object and a profession he truly loves.

It seems that I have been making knives all my life. As a boy, I made wooden swords and knives to play with and was designing them in high school. In 1952 I was inspired by the movie The Iron Mistress, *starring Alan Ladd as Jim Bowie, and how James Black made a huge knife for him. I was shocked when, at the end of the movie, Jim Bowie threw the knife into the river and it slowly sank to the bottom... I had to have a Bowie knife, so I made one!*
Knives are a passion for me. My greatest reward is in their creation. It seems like I step back and observe my inner-self working, I feel that I am in tune with the Divine Presence, and to this I owe the blessing of my creativity.

Opposite:
"The Dragonfly" 2003
The conceptual design for this creation is by Paul Ehlers. *"To mark our 20th year together as fantasy knife collaborators, Paul Ehlers and I decided to do a unique variation of our first design together".*
Grinding and polishing this piece presented a challenge for Gil; it required several different sizes of contact wheels. The fluted malachite handle adds a gracefully textured contrast to the mirror-polished 440C steel. The stainless steel pommel has two rubies, one inset on each side, to represent the Dragonfly's eyes. The shield is stainless steel and the spacers are file-worked nickel-silver and red metal.
Overall length 13 5/16" (338 mm).

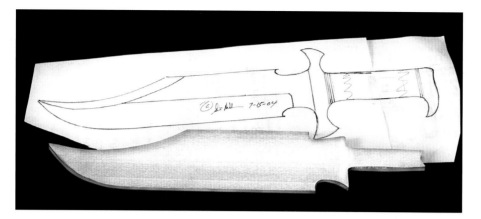

On the left:

Making the Bowie

Gil Hibben's skills were widely recognized in recent years when he designed the Rambo III knife for Sylvester Stallone, and with the success of that film came the success of that knife. Later he became associated with United Cutlery, resulting in many thousands of knives, factory-made to his design and specifications, selling throughout the world. But he still makes many custom art knives every year. Needless to say, as a young man making his first knife, never in his wildest dreams did he ever believe that stars such as John Wayne, Elvis Presley, Steve McQueen, Sylvester Stallone and Steven Segal, or world leaders such as Israel's Defense Minister Moshe Dayan and Vice-President Dan Quayle would one day own a Gil Hibben knife.

On the left is the Darom Bowie in the making, seen first with the sawed out blade ready for the grinding, laid out next to the original design-drawing of the knife. Below, Gil Hibben is seen concentrating on grinding the blade.

Opposite:

"Darom Bowie", 2004

"I wanted to make a Bowie with authority and yet have classic lines. I think this Bowie says it all!"
The 11" (280 mm) blade is of 440C stainless steel, the guard and pommel are stainless steel. The red coral handle takes this Bowie into the art world. 2 1/2" (63 mm) wide and 1/4" (6.3 mm) thick.

On the left:

"The Scorpion", 2001

"I enjoy taking knives to a futuristic level and this one did just that".
The handle is made of corian and has brass fittings, the steel is 440C. This knife was one of the prototypes Gil Hibben made for United Cutlery, who later went on to produce it as their 2001 annual Hibben Design Series. Overall length 15" (381 mm).

Opposite, from the left:

"Alamo Bowie", 2004

"I made my first knife of this design in 1966, while living in Manti, Utah. I am very honored to have a knife like this one permanently on display at the Alamo in San Antonio, Texas".
Gil copied an original American-made Bowie that was carbon dated back to the 1830s. The guard and blade catcher are of brass. The guard is stamped, as on the original, with stars and the initials J.B. The handle is of macassar ebony.
The 13 3/4" (349 mm) long 440C stainless steel blade is 2 1/2" (63 mm) wide and 1/4" (6.3 mm) thick. Overall length 19 3/4" (502 mm).

"The Iron Mistress", 2004

"I was absolutely passionate to make a knife like this after seeing the film The Iron Mistress *in 1952, starring Alan Ladd as Jim Bowie".*
The blade is of 440C stainless steel with a brass collar, butt cap and blade catcher. The ebony handle is inlaid with ivory and scrimshawed by Rick (Hutch) Hutchings.
The 10 1/2 " (267mm) long 440C stainless steel blade is 2" (51 mm) wide and 1/4" (6.3 mm) thick. Overall length 15 3/4" (400 mm).

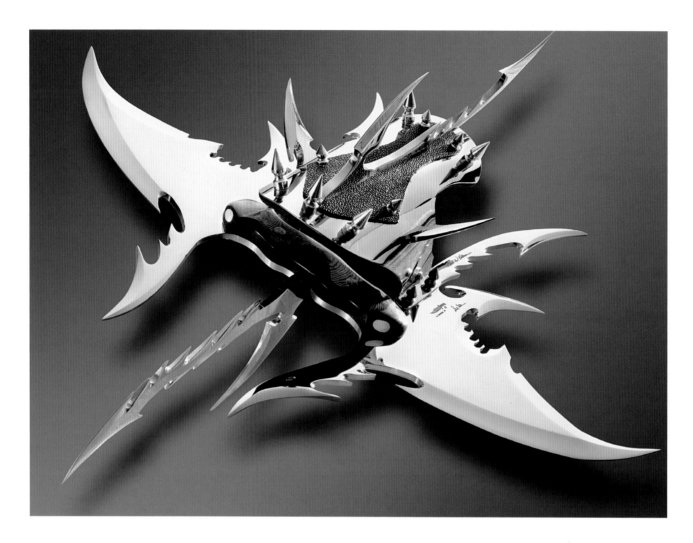

Above:

"The Stingray", 2002

Designed by Paul Ehlers, this piece took courage, determination and all the sheer strength Gil could muster or, as he puts it: *"Paul Ehler's dreams are my nightmares!!"* This multi-bladed creation, made of 440C steel, has hooks and barbs protruding in every direction. The upswept "wings" of the Stingray bring life to the piece and add a sense of gentle motion. The "eyes" are inlaid Mother-of-Pearl in the black micarta handle. And, of course, the inside of the grip and the spine are covered in stingray skin. Wing span 20" (508 mm).

Opposite, from the top:

"The Blade", 1999

"I was asked by a "movie knife" collector to make a knife similar to the one used in the film The Blade. *This is my take on that knife, it was another challenge to grind an unusual shape".*

The buffalo-horn handle is scrimshawed with the portrait of the movie's star, Wesley Snipes.
The scrimshaw was done by Rick (Hutch) Hutchings.
Overall length 13" (330mm).

"Mini Kahless", 2002

A small futuristic version of the classic *Star Trek* "Sword of Kahless". This one was an exercise in patience for Gil. The blade is of 440C stainless steel, the handle is black micarta with a file-worked back.
Overall length 17" (432 mm).

D'Alton Holder

Arizona, USA

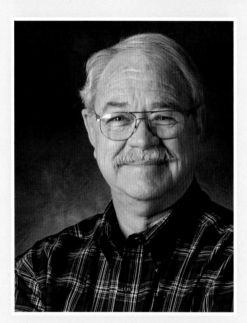

D'Alton Holder was born in Heald, Texas, in 1940. He attended high school in Amarillo, Texas and then went on to West Texas State University, graduating with degrees in Art and English Literature and a minor in Science. His next 25 years were spent in sales for an oil company, before he retired early in 1988 to become a full-time knifemaker. It was during his oil career that D'Alton got involved with custom knives. Like many talented people, he had an enjoyable hobby, and his was - building custom guns. It was when one of his gun customers asked him to make a knife to go along with his gun that he found his real place in the world. That was in Denver, Colorado, back in 1966, and that knife brought him all of $8. D'Alton truly sensed he had found his calling a few years later, after being transferred to Phoenix and meeting up with knifemakers Dan Dennehy and Don Wieler. Both of these early makers gladly shared ideas on equipment and construction techniques with D'Alton, and before he knew it, Dan invited him to join the Knifemakers Guild in July 1973 and attend their upcoming show in Kansas City, which he did. Three years later D'Alton was elected to the Guild's Board of Directors at the Las Vegas Guild Show, followed by two 2-year terms as President of the Guild. During the past 30 years D'Alton has also been active in local Arizona makers and collectors associations. Needless to say, this very talented gentleman has been recognized by his peers in many ways, receiving numerous honors and awards over the years. In 2003 he was a Knifemaker's Hall of Fame inductee.

D'Alton Holder, known commonly as D'Holder, or "Dee", works in a spacious shop in Phoenix, Arizona, where his specialty is making fancy using knives and an occasional Bowie just to keep things in balance. Currently, more than 75 custom makers worldwide give Dee credit for being a strong influence on their artistry. He claims he got far more from them than they got from him. That's probably true, as "students" often introduce design or construction elements the "teacher" never conceived of.

The manner in which I approach knifemaking is a combination of my art degree studies and 30 years in the oil business. Both artistic and practical. I believe that in order to succeed you first of all need to work hard. Second you must price your product fairly and honestly and make the best knife you can make. I try to take advantage of every minute I'm in the shop and have my equipment laid out in such a way that I could nail one foot to the floor and still finish a knife.

Opposite, from the top:
"Bird and Trout Knife", 2002
ATS-34 steel and 416 SS bolsters. The blade is a snick-blade with mammoth tooth handles and Pat Holder's engraving.
"Clip Blade Finger Groove", 2003
This model has under-handle bolsters engraved by Pat Holder. The handles are snowflake jade from Alaska. Blade is 4" (101 mm) long in ATS-34, the bolsters 416 SS.
"Drop-Point Finger Groove", 2003
This model has a 5" (127 mm) blade of ATS-34 steel and 416 SS side plates. The oval inlays are Picasso marble. Knife is engraved by Pat Holder.

Making the Handle

D'Alton Holder's knives are fancy in the sense that he uses top-quality handle materials and beautiful blade designs, many of them tastefully embellished with delicate engraving, thanks to the talent of his lovely wife, Pat. Like most artists, Pat received initial help from a good friend, in her case Julie Warenski, and during the past eight years she has gone on to develop her own engraving style. While Pat initially embellished knives by other makers, too, in recent years she has worked exclusively on Dee's knives.

The handle materials for the Musk Ox "My-Knife" were chosen for their natural beauty, their rarity, and the way they complement one another in contrast and color. All 41 parts of the handle are assembled, and between each layer there is a very thin bonding layer of epoxy. After drying completely, the whole mass is shaped by hand and eye to its final shape using increasingly fine grit abrasive until it is flat. The final stage is shaped at 1,200 grit. The entire handle is then buffed very lightly to bring out its color and shine. All this must be done so that the handle ends up smooth, flat and without any ripples despite the dissimilar materials. Then comes the toughest part: removing the butt cap for engraving without disturbing the other materials. After the engraving is completed, the butt cap is accurately re-installed and glued in place.

Opposite:

Musk Ox "My-knife", 2004
The blade is 4 1/4" (114 mm) long and made of ATS-34 stainless steel hardened to 61 Rc. It is mirror finished with a flawless shine. The fittings are nickel-silver. The handle is from some of the rarest materials around, the dominant element in the handle being stabilized Musk Ox horn from the Beaufort Sea area of the Arctic circle. The black spacers are fossil black whale bone, and the red is Fire Amber from the Baltic region of Europe. The scroll engraving was designed and executed by Pat Holder.

Above:

"Bear Knife", 2004

ATS-34 blade and nickel-silver fittings. The blade is 4" (101 mm) long. The handle is a combination of fossil narwal ivory and fossil walrus ivory. The scrimshaw, by Linda Karst-Stone, shows several bears and other forest animals, including the camp jay, trout, eagle, elk, and several others. The forward section of the handle is covered with prehistoric glyphs of native marine animals. The engraving and the relief bear carving are by Bruce Shaw.

Opposite, from the top:

"My-Knives", 2003

all with 4 1/4" (108 mm) blades.

Golden maple burl handle with bloodwood spacers and yellow amber. The blade is ATS-34 with nickel-silver guard and butt.

Golden maple handle with ebony spacers and yellow amber. Blade and fittings are nickel-silver.

Red maple with African blackwood spacers and red amber. Fittings are nickel-silver with a Damascus blade.

Oosic handle with African blackwood spacers and red amber. Blade is ATS-34 steel and fittings of nickel-silver. Engraving is scroll work by Pat Holder.

Above:

"Predator Series" Knives, 2004

The blades are ATS-34 steel and all have 416 stainless steel bolsters. The handles are select Mother-of-Pearl. The carvings are 18k gold coins set into the bolsters and carved in the likeness of several predatory animals, including the eagle, wolf and mountain lion. The blades are 4" (101 mm) long.

Opposite, from the top:

"Finger Groove", 2003

With Picasso marble handle. The blade is ATS-34 steel, bolsters 416 SS. The grizzly bear is done in deep relief by Bruce Shaw.

"Drop Point Finger Groove", 2002

With a 4" (101 mm) blade and bolsters of 416 SS. The blade is ATS-34. The Desert Bighorn sheep in relief carving is done by Bruce Shaw, the handle is Musk Ox horn, one the rarest handle materials in the world.

"Clip-Blade Finger Groove", 2002

With an ATS-34 steel blade and 416 SS bolsters. The handles are fossil mammoth tooth from Siberia. The grizzly engraving is done by Bruce Shaw.

"Drop Point Finger Groove", 2003

With an ATS-34 steel blade and 416 SS bolsters. The picture-frame grizzly is done in deep relief by Bruce Shaw. The handles are Musk Ox horn.

Paul M. Jarvis
Massachusetts, USA

Paul Jarvis was born in 1962 and resides in Cambridge, Massachusetts. Making knives since he was thirteen years old, he sold his first knife at the age of fifteen. His unique

talents arise from an inner passion to create beautiful objects and he has chosen knives and jewelry to do this. Paul started his apprenticeship as a mechanic during his second year at high school working for a company that manufactured laboratory equipment and dealt with material failure analysis. There he was involved in designing and making one-of-a-kind jigs and fixtures, using accurate machining tools and a variety of materials.

Twenty years later he began working for a company that sold industrial supplies, running their machine shop and, again, doing mostly one-of-a-kind highly specialized creative jobs.

Never having worked under any mentor, Paul is completely self-taught, influenced mainly by 18th-century Japanese metal artists as well as 17th- and 18th-century European craftsmen. His art also shows the influence of ancient Greek and classical Roman designs. His specialty is high relief carving, sculpting and background texturing using only hammers, chisels, punches and files. Sculpting his animal figures in gold or silver usually takes him many weeks of delicate carving. Gold, silver, bronze, exotic woods and various gems are his materials of choice. He tends to seek out rare materials for his unique pieces, making each one a very special and original work of art.

Paul does his art after work hours, every spare moment he has. Some of his knives may therefore take weeks or even many months to complete, ending up as extraordinary one-of-a-kind masterpieces. He usually makes no more than ten knives per year.

As long as I can remember I have always been artistic. As a child I could draw, paint, sculpt and carve, and I can now combine all these into each knife I make. I put my heart and soul into each piece, sharing a part of myself with the rest of the world within each creation of mine. I find great satisfaction in seeing the great passion in the eyes of those who buy my art. I then know that it will be treasured and preserved and be around for many generations to enjoy. It is my way to immortality.

Paul m Jarvis

Opposite:
"Mura Masa", 2004
The blade is made of a 64-layer single bar of Twisted Damascus by Daryl Meier, with carved grooves and Japanese Bonji figures. All fittings are carved and pierced Sterling silver set with 23 garnets in 14k gold bezels. Handle material is premium mammoth tooth. This knife, shown here from both sides, took Paul six months to complete.
Overall length 13" (330 mm).

Texturing Techniques

Paul does the indentations and stippling textures on his knives using a hammer and various types of punches. Texturing the bronze is done with a U-shaped punch of a very small edge diameter. The silver bezel is worked on with a needle-point punch. This is a very time consuming art, as each indentation is struck separately and with great care. Some of the tools Paul uses to create these visually exciting textures can be seen below.

Opposite:

"Kwaiken", 2003

The blade is made of a single bar of Twisted Damascus by Daryl Meier. Fittings are of sculpted and textured bronze that have been blackened and have polished raised rims. *Habaki*, guard and bezel are Sterling silver. Two 7 mm garnets are set in the bezel. Handle and scabbard are made of carved ivory.

"I finished the blade planning to make an European style dagger, using wood for the handle. Creating the habaki was so pleasing that I decided to complement it with ivory. The matching ivory scabbard actually took longer to make than the knife itself...".

Overall length 7 3/4" (196 mm).

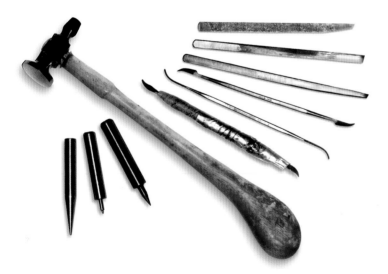

On the left:

"Glycerine", 1997

The 13" (330 mm) blade is made of double bar Twisted Damascus by Daryl Meier. The handle is mammoth ivory. The fittings are carved Sterling silver and bronze in high-relief designs with 24k gold inlays. Thirteen garnets and six peridot stones are set in 14k gold bezels. The sheath was made by Chris Kravitt. The four padded inlays (including the one behind the handle) are skins from the Malaysian horned frog. The detailing on the sheath duplicates the detailing in the gold and silver fittings on the knife. This art knife is the result of five months of Paul's craftsmanship.
Overall length 21" (533 mm).

Opposite:

"Kamakura", 1996

The blade is made of a single bar of Twisted Damascus by Daryl Meier, with carved grooves. All fittings are carved Sterling silver, and the carved silver peony blossoms in high relief have 24k gold inlays. Handle and scabbard are made of mammoth bone wrapped with 14k gold wire. This knife and scabbard took Paul seven months to complete.
Overall length 11 3/4" (298 mm).

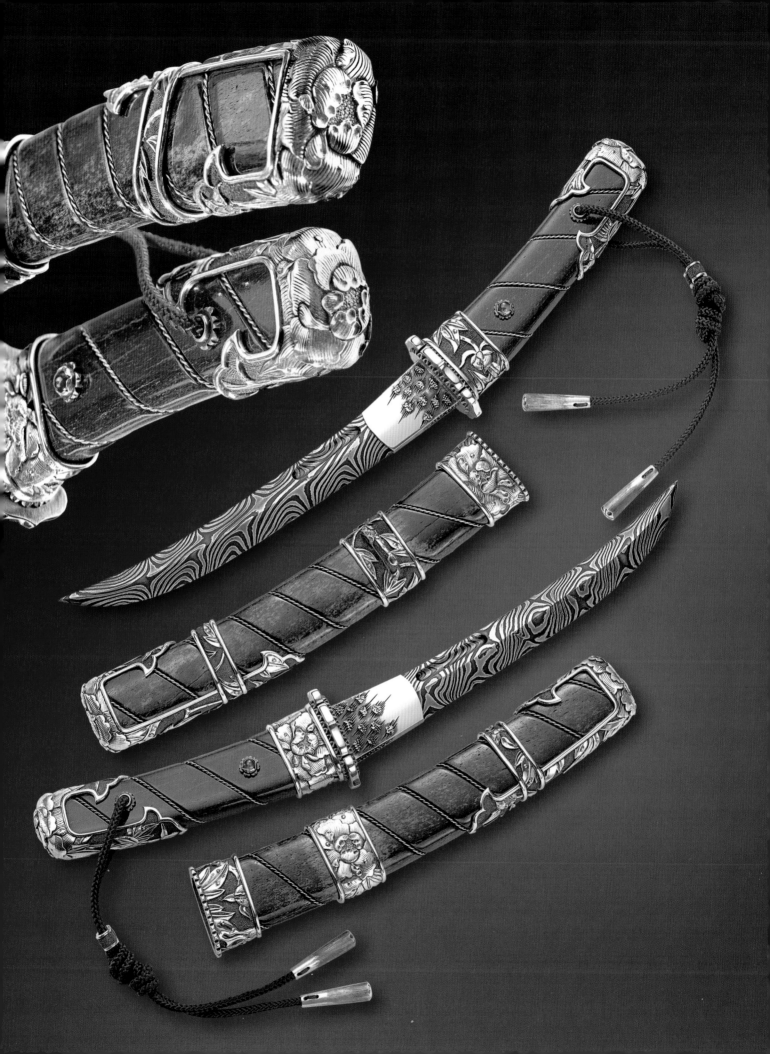

This page:
"Shimenwa Dagger", 2004
The 8" (203 mm) blade features
Daryl Meier's 64-layer Damascus.
The handle and scabbard are
carved ebony wood wrapped with
Sterling silver wire. The fittings are
carved Sterling silver set with two
amethysts. Two months from start to
finish.
*From the collection of Gerald Hopkin,
Barbados.*

Opposite:
"Topkapi Bowie", 1996
The 10 1/2" (267 mm) blade is
fabricated from 64-layer Damascus
by Daryl Meier. The mammoth ivory
handle features carved Sterling silver
augmented by twenty-two garnets
and eighteen tourmalines. Knife took
three months to complete. Sheath by
Chris Kravitt.
Overall length 18" (457 mm).

John L. Jensen
California, USA

John Jensen was born in Newport Beach, California, in 1971, and was raised in Los Angeles. Fascinated with both art and culture from an early age, John actively pursued these interests growing up. After graduating as valedictorian from his high school, he decided to indulge his passions full-time. His interests led him to study at the Savannah College of Art and Design, where he took his first classes in jewelry and sculpture. He later transferred to the Rhode Island School of Design, where he earned his BFA in jewelry and metalsmithing. Along the way he discovered knives - first through the creation of abstract sculpture, he then progressed onto the real thing.

In these modern times art is defined as a platform for ideas. The knife is where John exercises and expresses his thoughts on art, culture, sociology, archeology, anthropology and metaphor, all with stunning virtuosity. He has made admirable headway in his quest to merge the art and knife worlds. He is exhibiting more in galleries, as well as giving lectures and conducting workshops on knives. In the spring of 2004, John was a featured speaker at the Society of North American Goldsmiths annual conference, where his presentation "Art Knives: The Passion, the Quest, the Controversy" was well received by an audience of nearly 350. John has been featured in over 45 publications, nationally and internationally. His other artistic pursuits include painting, sculpture, photography, dance, theater, and writing. John works closely with his wife and business partner, Kristina, whom you'll find to be the beautiful face behind the table at the knife shows. John specializes in high-end, one-of-a-kind, collector art knives in his completely unique, unmistakable style. He is now working on a "how-to" DVD.

Fixed-blades are and have always been my first true love. They give me a much larger canvas to work on, which in turn gives me a larger palette to draw from. With fixed-blades, I'm not constrained by size, design, or mechanical movements. While all of my knives are made to the same exacting standards as those of a more traditional using knife, I really want my knives to be thought of, and viewed, as sculpture, as suitable for display as any other form of art. Overall, I enjoy raising questions and dumbfounding people with the complexity my knives.

John L. Jensen

Opposite:
"Krystallos", 2004
is a full-tang ATS-34 stainless steel creation, in which three different surface treatments and textures were employed. This knife has three important new and noticeable features. The bolsters are a result of two years of research; they are CP grade-2 titanium, showing the natural crystalline structure of this material. A natural golden beryl crystal, internally set, pierces through the entire thickness of the bolster area, which is rimmed in 18k royal yellow gold at the surface. The scales are premium-grade carved and rutilated Mother-of-Pearl. The "rutiles" are multiple layers of lacquered 22k Italian gold leaf. All of the gemstones are AAA-grade sapphires set in 18k royal yellow gold. Over 200 hours of labor. Overall length 18" (457 mm).

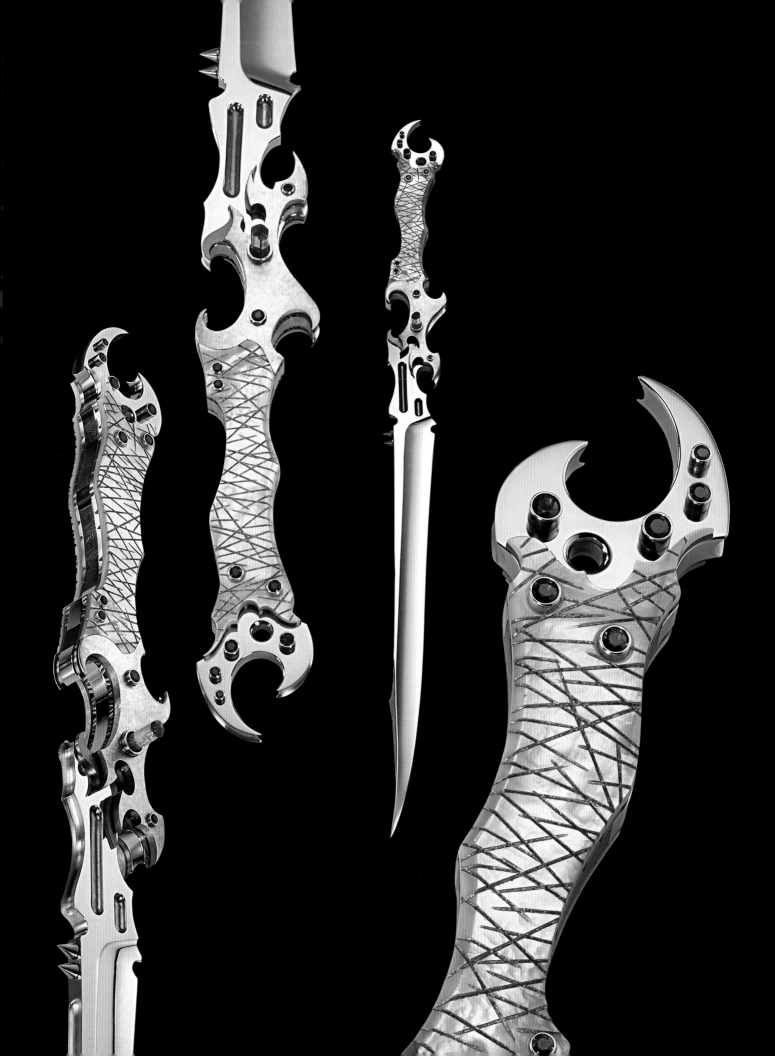

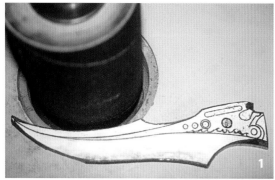

"At first glance people often mistake my fixed-blades for folders. This is due to the layering effect, materials and embellishment that I employ in the construction of all my knives. I like to cross the gap between what is happening with folders and fixed-blades. I enjoy my method of combining components. I can incorporate anodized titanium, layers, inlays, underlays, carving, cutaways, color, depth and dimension with an unending supply of material combinations and treatments. I do also want people to know that aside from using Damascus from many different makers, I do forge and use my own Damascus steel as well".

On the left:

Making the Blade for "Strata Dragon"

1 The rough-cut profiled blade is now sanded to the exact, final smooth-finished profile on an oscillating spindle sander, this machine keeps my profiles at exactly 90°.

2 Hollow-grinding the blade with a 5" (127 mm) wheel on my "Burr King". Starting with an 80 grit belt, then moving up to finer grits: 120, 220, 320, 400, 600, and finally, 800 or higher.

3 Heat-treating the blade consists of bringing the blade up to 1,500°F, quickly quenching in oil, then tempering for an hour at about 350°F. Repeating the process if necessary.

4 Acid etching of the blade. Areas not to be etched can be masked off with nail polish; this can also be used as a decorative effect, as I have done here with the small flame pattern at the top of the grind on the ricasso. Depending on the Damascus, I generally take my steel to an 800 grit finish, buff, then etch in 10-minute increments, scrubbing the surface with a fine brush in the solution during the process. This procedure is repeated until the desired depth of etch is achieved. I then go through a three-step neutralizing process: TSP (tri-sodium phosphate), baking soda and distilled water, and finally ammonia contained in a glass cleaner. Any nail polish is then removed.

5 Final polishing using a small hand held "Foredom" flex shaft in preparation for hot-bluing.

Opposite:

"Strata Dragon", 2004

"With "Strata Dragon" I really delved into the theme of fantasy that one could very easily build a story line around. This piece is very sculptural, dimension-wise, with its protruding, flaring solid gold horns and gold piercings. This is also my first use of carbon fiber. Damascus steel is by Gary House, hot-blued with polished ricasso, bolsters are heat-colored meteorite. Liners, spikes and handle core are all anodized titanium. Inlays consist of abalone, mokume-gane, my signature logo and a photo under semi-transparent pearl". This knife won the Best Fantasy award at the 2004 Blade Show as well as the award for the overall Best Fantasy Knife of 2004. It was also on display in 2004, at the Center Arts Gallery, Grand Rapids, Michigan, in a show entitled "Hammer & Hand: Contemporary American Metal". 115 hours of labor.

Overall length 14" (356 mm).

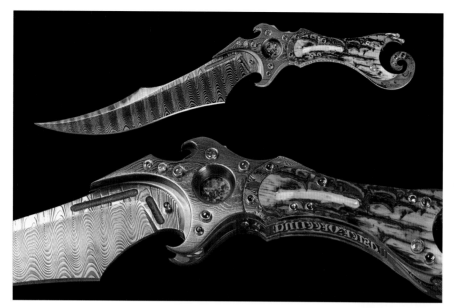

On the left:

"Virtual Velocity", 2003

This knife incorporates several new techniques and concepts, adding many unique, and almost hidden, details. The blade is a very bold, highly chatoyant Ladder pattern Damascus forged by Daryl Meier with milled accents, deep-etched and hot-blued to a deep purple, with hints of blue and bronze as well as a polished ricasso. The bolsters are in two parts, incorporating two different Damascus patterns and finish treatments; the second has its own set of two-layer "liners". Along the top spine is another of John's signature inlays - a photo of a mysterious, beautiful woman's face appearing from within the transparent shell. Along the bottom of the handle you can glimpse a large Sterling silver inlay that was once the face of a stamp John found at a flea market. 185 hours of labor. Overall length 13 1/2" (343 mm).

Opposite, from the left:

"Cyclops", 2004

This knife features an incredible Twisted Basket Weave Mosaic, Candy-Stripe pattern Damascus blade forged by George Werth, and pure nickel, with milled accents. The offset grind, and other asymmetrical elements, are a unique twist on the classic dagger form. The bolsters are heat colored, twisted Mosaic Damascus. The thematic point of this knife is a glass taxidermy crocodile eye set in 18k gold. In keeping with the "Cyclops" theme, there is only one of these. The scales are a unique composite of laminated layers of natural Black-Lip Pearl, creating a layered and pooling effect when contoured. The reverse side of the handle features a very unique design element called an "Ambigram", designed by John Langdon - a word that reads the same way right side up and upside down! In this case, the name of the knife, "Cyclops". The gemstones are all set in 18k yellow gold. 140 hours of labor. Overall length 15 1/2" (mm).

"Invocation", 1999

This knife gets its name from the concept of conjuring up spirits. The blade is a one-of-a-kind, deeply hollow-ground, deeply etched 3-bar composite, low-layer, Loose Twist Damascus, forged by Daryl Meier. The handle took three templates to make, as the various components are all of different shapes: anodized and carved titanium tang wrap, file-worked titanium liners, and colored, impregnated and stabilized maple burl scales. A total of 26 gemstones set in 18k yellow gold are deliberately sprinkled throughout the handle to compliment all textures and colors. There are nearly 40 hidden screws in this piece. Overall length 15 1/2" (394 mm).

"Voodoo Child", 1998

To avoid covering the beautiful Damascus of this Integral, John welded a steel tang onto the blade and fit a titanium slab around it, connecting all of this internally via hidden screws. He inlaid copper-nickel mokume-gane over the seam where the blade steel meets the titanium tang wrap. The bolsters and fossil mastodon ivory meet in a dovetailed joint. The pommel is patterned and features large bi-color andulusites and garnets set in 14k white gold. The slightly offset grind of the blade was done intentionally to match the main visual line in the Mosaic bolsters. Liners are file-worked, anodized titanium. Overall length 9" (228 mm).

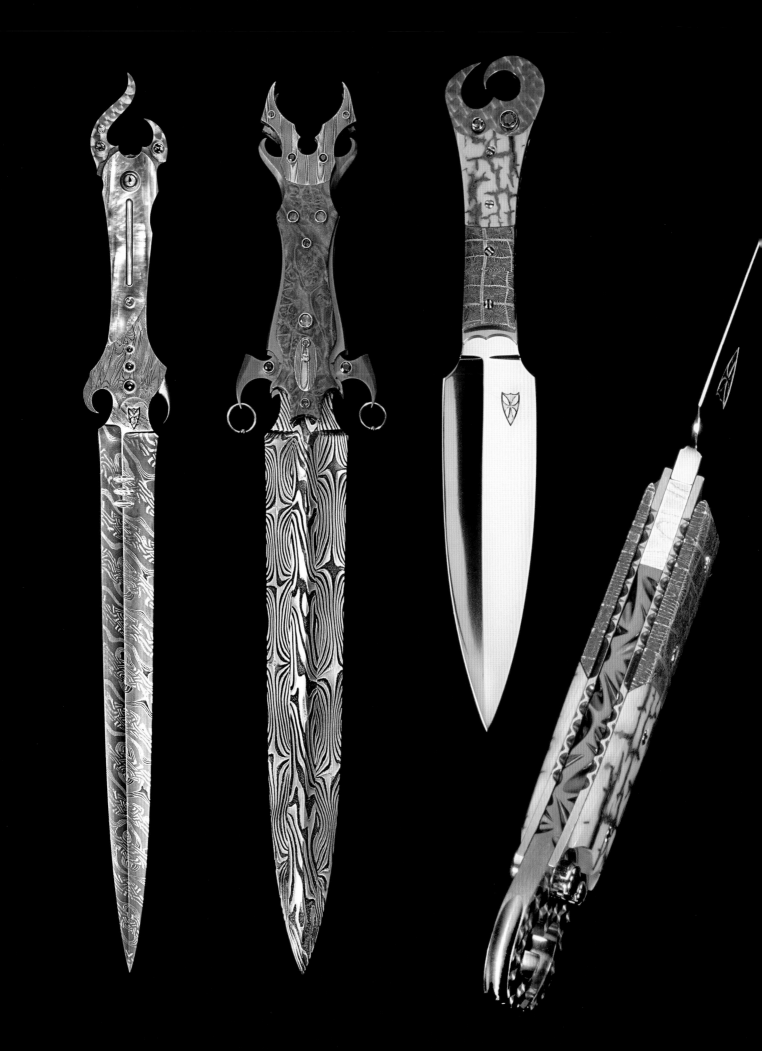

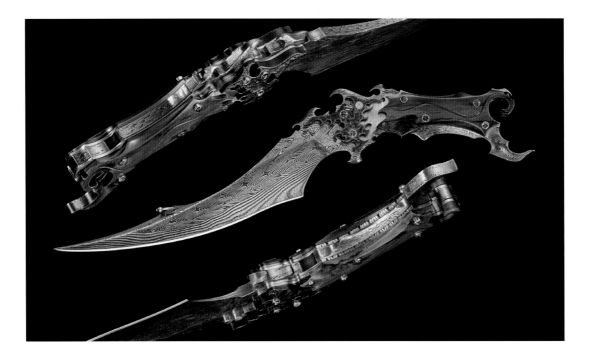

Above:

"Infernos Vertigo", 2001

This was a commissioned piece. John and his client agreed on a "fire" theme, which was explored not only though shapes but also through material choices. The blade is a 3-layer sandwich, "San Mai", using two different Damascus patterns. The Twist pattern Damascus bolsters were carved in an undulating way, to mimic fire, then deeply etched and colored in shades of plum with hints of blue. This was the most time consuming and tedious single element John has worked on to date. They were cut and shaped with only a jeweler's saw, and small grinding bits, set up in a drill press. The Damascus was forged by Daryl Meier. Titanium bolster liners are also shaped in the form of fire under the bolster area, though slightly oversized for a ghosting effect. Gemstones front to back, all set in 18k yellow gold bezels. 250 hours of labor. Overall length 12 1/4" (311 mm).

Opposite, from the left:

"Stallion Talon", 2000

The forging process you see on the blade is a 3-layer sandwich called "San Mai". Here the outsides are Turkish Twist Damascus, and the center core is high-grade tool steel. All of the steel, including the Ladder pattern bolsters, was forged by Daryl Meier. The titanium handle core and liners feature two-color anodizing and texturing. The handle material is gorgeous sky blue, white and orange fossil walrus ivory. This was the first knife in which John used the semi-transparent pearl with his logo and picture on the spine. Stones from front to back. 175 hours of labor. Overall length 13 1/2" (343 mm).

"Synchronicity", 2004

A small and elegant executive's desk knife featuring a blade of accordioned Mosaic Damascus steel with a composite twist cutting edge, forged by Johan Gustafsson. Deep-etched and heat-colored, with milled accents and polished ricasso. Stones from front to back set in 18k royal yellow gold. The spine features three abalone inlays, heat-colored Gibeon meteorite, a semi-transparent shell inlay with cropped face picture underlay, as well as a semi-transparent shell with John's signature logo underlay. 85 hours of labor.
Overall length 8 1/2" (216 mm).

"Echoes Desire", 1999

The Damascus blade was forged and shaped to John's specifications by Conny Persson. The handle consists of anodized titanium liners that feature intricate file work and bevels. The bolsters are a 6-bar composite Turkish Twist Damascus by Daryl Meier. The scales are fossilized Siberian mastodon ivory in shades of green, blue, brown, and cream. Eighteen semi-precious stones set in 18k gold highlight and accent the whole ensemble. Gemstones cover all of the external construction screws. Overall length 11" (279 mm).

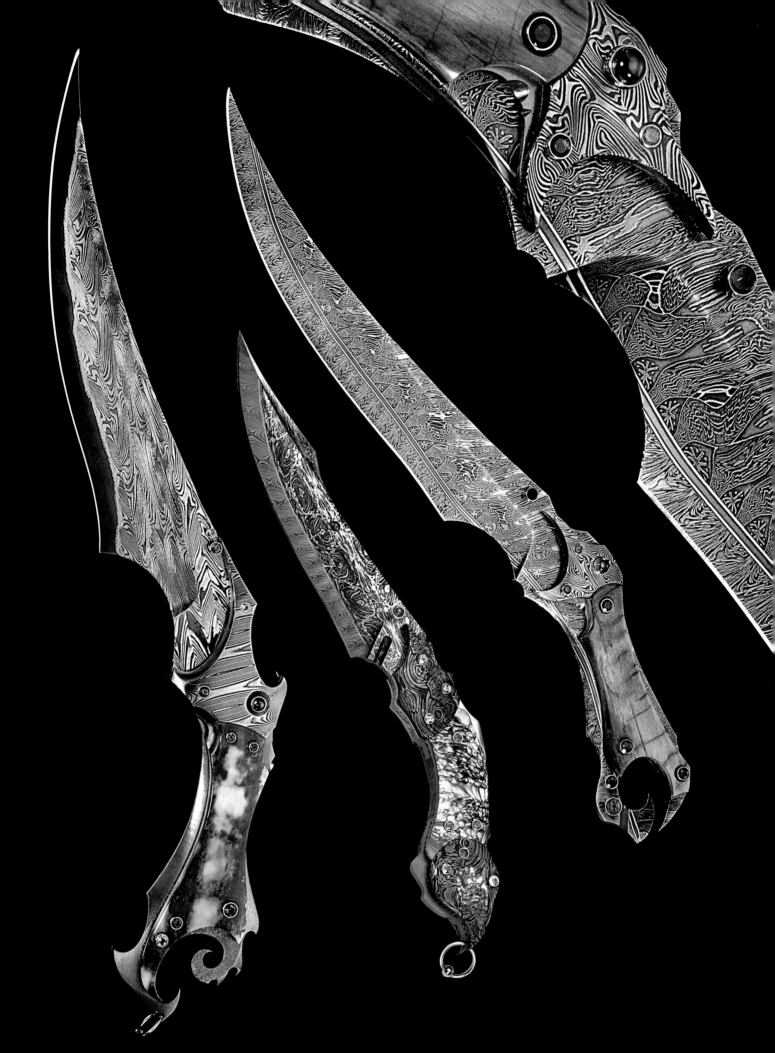

Steve R. Johnson
Utah, USA

For Steve, born in 1948, growing up in a small town in south-central Utah, USA, was a great experience. He had the opportunity to hunt, fish, ride horses, camp, play ball, and work on his father's farm for most of his years as a youth. A natural part of life for a boy in Manti included membership in the Boy Scouts of America, of which he still is a member. This turned out to influence his whole life, because that's where he was introduced to the custom knife. Steve was very fortunate to have Gil Hibben as his Boy Scout Explorer Advisor, and when Gil gave each scout the opportunity to make a knife in his shop, Steve jumped at the chance. His first knife was completed in March 1966. He still has that knife, made from forged 440C, and has used it many times. For him, that "project" evolved into part-time and then full-time work. He also had the opportunity to work with great knifemakers such as Harvey Draper, Rod Chappel, Buster Warenski and, thanks to the kind recommendation of long-time friend and advisor A. G. Russell, with Bob Loveless also.

Knifemaking has remained a constant in Steve's life, and he enjoys the people and places associated with knifemaking and the personal challenge of making each knife. Steve is a member of the Italian Knifemakers Guild and the Professional Knifemakers Association, and he presently serves on the Knifemakers' Guild Board of Directors as Secretary/Treasurer and enjoys his association with the Board and the many great members of the Guild and the knifemaking community, worldwide. He still sees it as a privilege to work in the custom knife business and is very thankful for the experiences he has had and for the wonderful friends and acquaintances, throughout the world, which have resulted from 38 years in the knifemaking field.

Steve and his wife, Dorothy, are parents of three daughters and four sons who are a source of great happiness to both of them.

I cannot pinpoint what intrigued me so much when I was handed that first Hibben custom hunter back in 1965, but I knew I would own a knife like that some day! Was it the solid feel, the fit and finish, the keen edge, the polished blade, the handle material? Surely, it was a combination of all these things. And it is still difficult to explain. Back then, I never dreamed that oneday I'd make my living crafting knives. The knife has a certain mystique that rings true in almost any person. This is especially true when it is a custom-made knife that has been created by a master knifemaker. The concept of the custom knife, though centuries old, is new, and with today's talented artisans, I feel that there is no limit to where this art form will take us. It has been a privilege for my family and me to work in this business!

S. R. Johnson

Opposite, from the left:
New York ECCKS Knives, 2004
"Loveless-style Boot Knife",
5 1/4" (133 mm) blade, stainless steel fittings, bark Cape Buffalo horn handles.
Overall length 9" (228 mm).
"Loveless-style Wilderness",
5" (127 mm) blade stainless steel fitting. Desert Ironwood handles.
Overall length 10" (254 mm).
"Cottontail", 3 1/4" (82 mm) blade with clip bevel grind, stainless steel fitting. Snakewood handles.
Overall length 7 1/4" (184 mm).

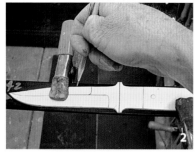

On this left:

Making the Blade

1 After planning the design for a new knife, it is accurately drawn out.

2 When drawing the design has been completed, the pattern is cut out and then glued onto stiff cardboard, plastic or even steel, for transferring its outline to the knife steel. The new "template" is then stored for future use when making knives of this same pattern.

3 After transferring (or scribing) the pattern onto the bar of steel, in this case BG-42, the knife is sawn out on a slow-speed band-saw.

4 The guideline for the knife's edge is scribed along the edge of the sawn-to-shape knife blank. A line for the center line is also scribed on both sides of the blade.

5 Grinding the blade's bottom bevel is done on an 8" (203 mm) wheel, prior to heat treating.

6 The blade has been cooled in a nearby water container before continuing with the top grind of the rough grinding stage, on a 3" (76 mm) wheel.

7 As usual, this Classic Fighter's blade was also ground edge-up, allowing close supervision of the edge. For the top bevel, a 3" (76 mm) wheel was used. Steve generally holds the handle edge of the knife with his bare hand and uses a glove to hold the blade end, where the heat is generated. He feels that this gives him more control.

Opposite page

"David's Fighter", 2004

Based on the design of Steve's Classic Fighter marked # 001. This knife has a 5.5" (140 mm), clipped blade, featuring T-416 stainless steel bolsters, handle screws and pins. Premium Mother-of-Pearl handles and his Classic-Series thong slot at the rear of the handle. Custom-made basket-stamped leather sheath, by Nate Christensen, saddle maker. For strength and a pleasing appearance, the top grind is terminated forward of the bottom grind by about 5/8" (16 mm). The top grind was done on a 3" (76 mm) grinding wheel, the bottom grind on an 8" (203 mm) wheel, giving the bottom edge more strength and the top edge more sharpenability. Overall length 10 3/8" (263 mm).

On the left:

AKI Knives, 2003

"There's not much of a connection between the four knives I made for the 2003 AKI show, but I usually try to come up with something different for this show. The Classic Dagger is a symmetrical version of my Classic Fighter with nice big bolsters for possible engraving, and premium Sambar stag that is quite scarce these days. The Sykes-Fairbairn is a knife that I've long wanted to make, spruced up with some gold. The gold bolstered New York Special is what I consider to be the ultimate high-society personal protection blade. Gold automatically adds class, as does the quite rare and beautiful Cape Buffalo horn. The little Integral caper is what I consider to be a perfect "Gent's Knife". The Integral construction, along with MOP make it pretty much impervious to the moisture and temperature effects that would normally be encountered by such a knife. The logo was put in that position to make it unique".

"Sykes-Fairbairn-type Commando Dagger"
14k gold guard, gold-plated pommel, African blackwood handle, 7 1/4" (184 mm) blade. Overall length 12" (305 mm).

"Classic Dagger #001"
5" (127 mm) blade, stainless steel fitting, Sambar stag. Overall length 10" (254 mm).

"Loveless-style New York Special"
3 1/2" (89 mm) blade, 14k gold bolsters, Cape Buffalo handles. Overall length 7 1/4" (184 mm).

"Caper"
Integral, Mother-of-Pearl handle slabs. Overall length 6" (152 mm).
All four knives are made of ATS-34 steel.

Opposite, from the left:

"Millennium Knife", 2000
Sub-Hilt with hidden tang. Made to celebrate the new millennium, it carries a special trademark and the date - 01.01.2000 on one side of the blade and three logos previously used by Steve Johnson in his knifemaking career on its reverse side. The knife has a double-edged Loveless-style fighter blade, with a "swell" in the cutting edge, and has a double guard with a swept-back appearance. The stag handle is capped on the end with a stainless steel end plate. Overall length 11 27/64" (290 mm).

Knives made from designs of other knifemakers:

"Rigid Knife", 1996
Made after an interesting and very rugged design by Rigid Company. Bark stag handle. Overall length 8 15/16" (227 mm).

"Cooper Sub-Hilt", 1996
"I met John Nelson Cooper when I first arrived in Los Angeles, California, to work with Bob Loveless. I've long remembered that meeting. It was very enjoyable to make a knife following the design of his Sub-Hilt Bowie".
Polished stag handle. Overall length 12" (306 mm).
All three knives from the collection of Dr. Pierluigi Peroni, Italy.

On the left:

"Sub-Hilt Bowie", 1999

This large "One-of-a-kind," Sub-Hilt Bowie measures a full 16" (390 mm) overall with a 9 3/4" (230 mm) ATS-34 blade 1/4" (6.3 mm) thick. T-416 fittings and fossilized walrus ivory handle of hidden-tang construction, with finger grooves. The clip-point Bowie blade is magnificently engraved by the world-renowned Firmo Fracassi of Brescia, Italy. The "African Big Five" motif on the right side of the blade displays a tranquil African scene featuring the elephant, Cape Buffalo, rhinoceros, lion and leopard. Firmo Fracassi also engraved the maker's name on the left side of the blade, bordered with a beautiful floral scroll.

Opposite, from the left:

Five Collaboration Knives

"Loveless–Johnson Set of Three", 1994

A "Fighter", a "Utility" and a "Chute" with premium well-matching stag handles, after designs by Bob Loveless. All knives carry the "Loveless & Johnson" trademark, each also marked "PROTOTYPE" on the ricasso.

"Kressler–Johnson Boot Knife", 1996

The only Full-Integral, asymmetrical Boot Knife, made in a collaboration between Dietmar Kressler (Germany) and Steve Johnson. Exotic-wood handle. Overall length 9 5/16" (236 mm).

"Johnson–Velarde Hide-Out", 1999

Full-Integral, made in a collaboration between Ricardo Velarde (USA) and Steve Johnson. Stag handle and serial numbered "001".

All five knives from the collection of Dr. Pierluigi Peroni, Italy.

Dietmar Kressler
Odelzhausen, Germany

Born in 1946, in Bremen, Germany, Dietmar Kressler began making knives as a hobby in 1971, during his military service. Later he went on to study mechanical engineering in Cologne, but making knives remained his chief obsession. In 1985 Dietmar quit his job to become a full-time knifemaker. He received help and guidance from Bob Loveless and A. G. Russell, but soon developed his own style, making mainly Integral knives and a few Interframes. He sold his first knife, a drop-point hunter with a guard and wooden handle, for $35. Fifteen years later he had the opportunity to buy this first knife back and gladly payed $1,250 for it. He has kept it in his treasured possession ever since.

Dietmar's first Full-Integral knife, a Semi-Skinner finished in 1982, is now considered a rare and historic collector's item. It is shown here on page 202. About one of his other first designs he says: *"The first Integral Sub-Hilt Fighter I made was a unique moment in my career, and it probably cannot be copied in the same way by any other maker. Making this type of knife still gives me great satisfaction".*

An important element in his knifemaking is choosing the right steel to work with and selecting the best handle material for each knife. The overall high quality and the typical "Kressler look" of his knives have brought him many awards at international knife shows. He prefers making knives with no engraving, scrimshaw or precious metal embellishing, just straightforward practical designs, created with great accuracy and with a perfect combination of the best stee, excellent edge retention and premium handle materials. This is also the great appeal his knives have for collectors. Dietmar himself loves it most when they actually put his knives to use, often sending them back to him for resharpening.

Just making a high-quality knife doesn't make an artist out of a knifemaker. It is the ability to feel and create new things in a knife, not necessarily changing its shape but giving it a new look even by working new contrasts in its finish, that elevates a knifemaker to a higher level.

Opposite, from the left:
"Big Bear", 2000
A Full-Integral *Big Bear* with surface Desert Ironwood handle.
Overall length 13 3/4" (350 mm).
"Fighter", 1999
A Full-Integral *Fighter* with premium snakewood handle.
Overall length 11 1/2" (292 mm).
"Chute", 1986/1987
The first Full-Integral *Chute* created by Dietmar Kressler. Handle material is dark Desert Ironwood.
Overall length 9 2/5" (234 mm).
"Millennium Knife", 2000
This was Dietmar's first knife for the new millennium. It has a unique logo with the year 2000 in the center. The reverse side of the blade is marked "01-01-2000". A Full-Integral hunting knife of a completely new design and black micarta handle. The handle is attached to the knife by two stainless steel tubes.
Overall length 9 2/5" (239 mm).
All four knives from the collection of Dr. Pierluigi Peroni, Italy.

On the left:
Making a Semi-Integral
1-4 Dietmar Kressler is seen here working on some of the most common stages in creating a Semi-Integral: measuring the width of the blade at the ricasso, just in front of the guard; carefully shaping and polishing the front guard; drilling; grinding the shape of the knife using an 18" contact wheel.

5 Over the years Dietmar has developed close relationships with knifemakers around the world and wonderful friendships with many of his collector clients. *"It is a very unique situation, as the relationships established with almost all of my clients have developed into deep and long-lasting friendships".* Kressler is seen here with his friend Dr. Pierluigi Peroni (in the middle) and with American knifemaker and friend of many years, Ron Lake.

Opposite:
"Utility Lamb", 2004
This perfectly balanced Semi-Integral has in it all the typical elements of a Kressler hand-made knife that is meant to be used, and used for many years, at home or in the field.
The simplicity of its lines and its practical design are combined with a perfect finish using premium materials. The handle is made of two matching stag slabs.
Overall length 7" (178 mm).

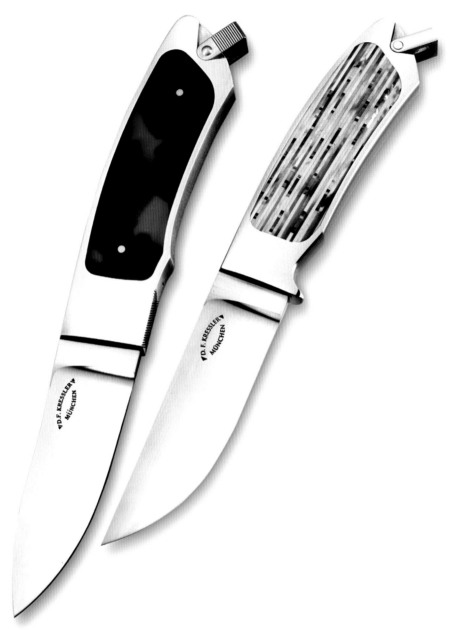

On the left:
"Tortoise Shell Interframe",
1985/1986
A classic knife, this is the first
Interframe knife to leave Kressler's
workshop. It has tortoise shell inlays
and a 3" (78 mm) blade.
Overall length 6 7/8" (175 mm).
"Interframe Skinner", 2001
Made for the 2001 Art Knife
Invitational Show (AKI) in San Diego,
this is a collaboration with Jurgen
Steinau, whose extraordinary style is
quite obvious in the construction of
the handle.
Overall length 7" (180 mm).
Both knives from the collection of
Dr. Pierluigi Peroni, Italy.

Opposite, from the left:
Lake - Kressler Collaborations
Two "Symmetrical Daggers",
1995-1997
These are the only two existing
knives made in a collaboration
between Dietmar Kressler and Ron
Lake (USA). Kressler made the blades
of these Integrals, in Ron's typical
Symmetrical Boot Knife design. Ron
Lake made the handles and finished
the knives. The handles are premium
quality stag. Both knives of this
perfectly matching set are 8 7/8"
(276 mm) long.
From the collection of Dr. Pierluigi
Peroni, Italy.

On the left:

"Semi-Skinner", 1981/1982

This is Kressler's first Integral knife, making it a rare and historic collector's item. The knife is fully engraved by Manfred Fleischer and has the original "Loveless Design" trademark used by Kressler at the beginning of his career as a knifemaker.

Overall length 8 3/16" (207 mm).

From the collection of Dr. Pierluigi Peroni, Italy.

Opposite:

"PLP City Knife", 1998

This small Full-Integral knife was made especially for its owner, the Italian collector Dr. Pierluigi Peroni, and is therefore also monogramed "PLP". It is fully engraved by Stanley Stoltz and has a premium Mother-of-Pearl handle.

Overall length 5 7/8" (151 mm).

From the collection of Dr. Pierluigi Peroni, Italy.

Francesco Pachì
Sassello, Italy

Francesco Pachì was born in 1961, in Genoa, Italy. Today he lives in Sassello, Italy, in inland Liguria, in a house surrounded by woods and meadows, with his wife, Mirella, and his daughter, Gaia, now eight years old. After finishing his scientific studies, in 1983, he started a publicity photography company that within a few years became one of the most successful in the city of Genoa. Forever a lover of nature and outdoor activity as well as an expert archer and hunter, he began his approach to the world of knives. In 1991 Pachì became deeply interested in steels and the components used in creating them. Completely self-taught, he began his first experiments with grinding, which led him, in 1994, to his first exhibition. In 1995, after a trip to the United States and a few days spent in the studio of the great American master Steve Johnson, he decided to devote himself full-time to knifemaking, thus making it his primary occupation.

At the beginning, his main clients were archers and hunters, and the knives were mainly practical hunters and skinners. Then, once he made contact with the world of collectors, his style, designs and finish grew more sophisticated, featuring beautiful visual balance and impeccable workmanship, remaining, however, functional as ever. The special characteristic of his blades is without doubt the chipped appearance of the flat of the blade, creating a pleasant contrast to the perfectly polished, mirror-like finish of the blade. This trademark is found in every knife Francesco makes, whether in steel or Damascus, fixed-blade or folder. Many of his creations are finished using fossil ivory for the handles, both mammoth and walrus, on which his wife, Mirella, a well known scrimshaw artist, engraves true masterpieces.

I remember having always enjoyed making things with my hands, giving shape to a design or matching two objects of different form and color in an attempt to find a balanced composition. Over the years, all this has led me to make photography my profession, without a doubt, the most influential factor in my professional life. I remember long days spent building sets, painting backgrounds and inventing mechanisms to be used in photo sessions, always with Mirella, my wife, nearby to give me a hand with her vast experience in graphic design and advertising. Making knives for me and doing scrimshaw engraving for her was an important choice in our lives and an intense experience. For me, making a knife is still like putting together a photo set, with that subtle balance between volumes, colors and dexterity, all of which are necessary to create an object in which the fine line between workmanship and art disappears.

Opposite, from the left:
"Two Daggers and a Boot Knife", 1998-1999
Knife on the left, made of stainless Rose pattern Damascus from Damasteel, has two opals in the handle. The other two are of stainless Ladder pattern Damascus by Devin Thomas. Bolsters engraved with gold inlays by Salvatore Panteghini. All handles are abalone shell.
Overall lengths 10 13/16" (275 mm), 9" (230 mm) and 8 9/16" (220 mm).

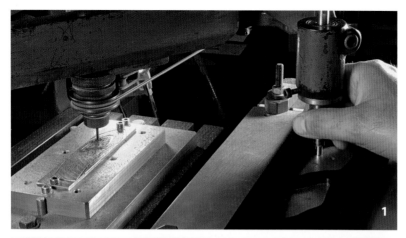

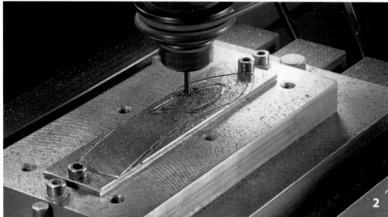

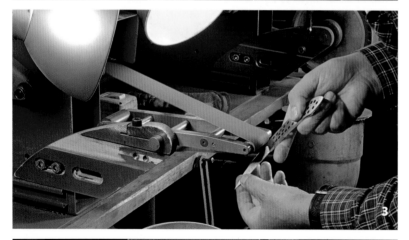

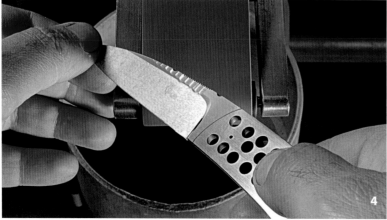

On the left:
Making a Utility Knife
1-2 Working with a pantograph to mill the interframe pockets on the 416 stainless steel handle slabs.
3-4 Francesco Pachi creating his trademark chipping on the flat of the blade using a small wheel on the grinder while being very careful not to ruin the finish of the blade.

Opposite:
"Utility Knife", 2004
Utility knife made of RWL-34 stainless steel with scales made of 416 stainless steel. Double interframe inserts of blued carbon Damascus steel. Anodized titanium liners. Overall length 7 13/16" (199 mm).

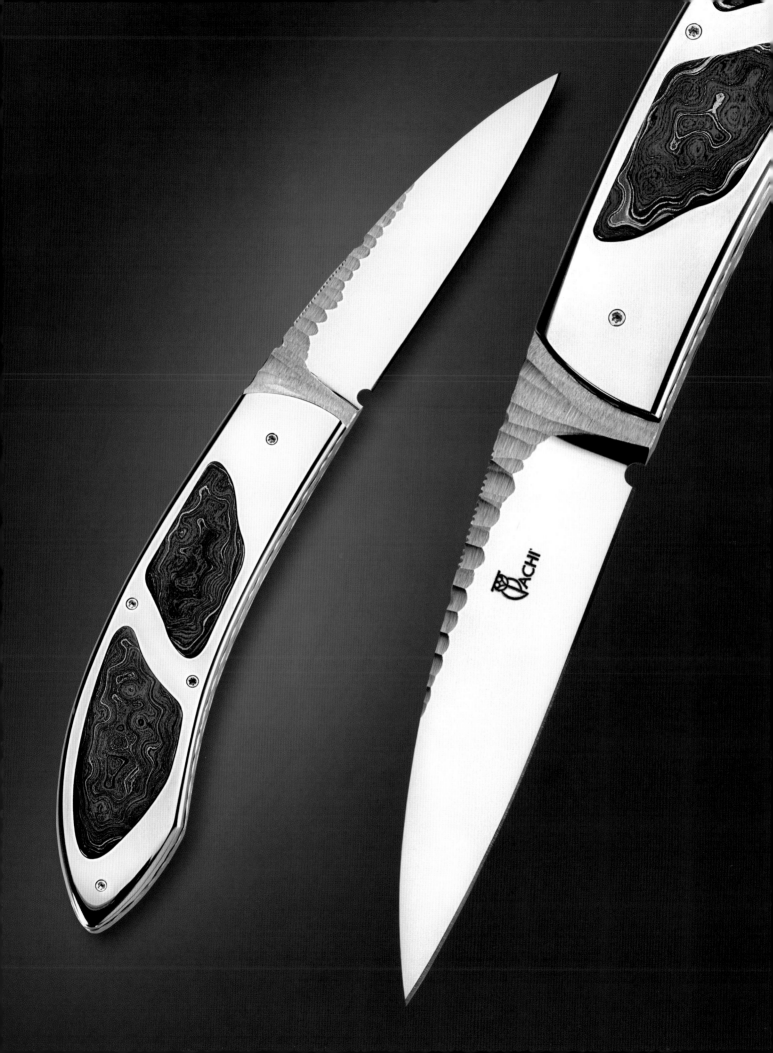

This page:
"Tribal Boot Knife", 2002
Blade made of blued carbon Mosaic
Damascus from Bob Eggerling,
carbon steel scales with gold inlay by
V. Zanettti.
Overall length 8 9/16" (220 mm).

Opposite, from the left:
Two "Huntmasters", 1999 and 2001
Two hunting knives with blades
made of carbon Damascus by D.
Meier (left) and D. Thomas. Bolsters
engraved with gold inlay and
chisel work by S. Panteghini. White
Mother-of-Pearl scales sculpted by
S. Panteghini and mammoth ivory
scales with scrimshaw by Mirella
Pachi. Overall length of both knives
11 3/8" (290 mm).

On the left:

Two "Luna" City Knives, 1999
A matching pair of city knives made of stainless steel Rose pattern Damascus by D. Thomas, Mosaic pins and mammoth ivory scales scrimshawed by Mirella Pachi. Overall length 6 5/16" (160 mm).

Opposite:

"Pro Hunter - Big Five", 2004
Blade made of RWL-34 stainless steel. Scales made of 416 stainless steel with five interframe inserts of mammoth ivory, scrimshaw by Mirella Pachi, depicting the African Big-Game Five. Anodized titanium liners. Overall length 10 7/16" (265 mm). *From the collection of Dr. Pierluigi Peroni, Italy.*

Conny Persson
Los, Sweden

Conny Persson, born in 1964. has been living in Los, a town in the far north of Sweden, for most of his life. After graduating as a mechanical engineer and finishing his military service in the navy, he returned to Los and took up the production of whetstones, a business his great-grandfather began in 1870. It was in 1991 that he was introduced to custom knives, when he purchased a knife with a Damascus blade. So impressed was Conny, that he began experimenting with steel and making Random and Twist Patterned Damascus blades which he sold to Swedish knifemakers. Soon after, in 1994, he read an article dealing with Mosaic Damascus, and again he was completely captivated. Thus began a period in his life where he spent weeks on end developing his own designs and techniques while learning the long and precise multi-stage processes involved in creating wonderful Mosaic designs. Looking back at this exciting period in his life, he recognizes that he had created Mosaic patterns that were way beyond what he ever imagined was actually possible. In 1997 Conny attended his first of what would be many knife show in the USA, and he has since attended many European and Scandinavian shows, introducing his artistry to collectors from around the world. Amongst these shows are the ECCKS in New York, the Blade Show and the Italian Milan Show.

Many of his Mosaic patterns are so intricate, so beautiful, collectors realize he spent perhaps weeks or months assembling different blanks and components before even starting the time-consuming hard work of forge-welding all the pieces together without distorting their original patterns. It is at this point, when one examines knives such as these, that all the skills involved come to light. Needless to say, Conny constantly strives to reach higher artistic levels with every new pattern he creates. The materials he uses for his knives are only from natural sources, and he is especially fond of fossilized materials for his handles.

When I work on a new Mosaic pattern I always try to get it as perfect as possible. The best and most exciting moment for me is the stage where I dip the steel into an acid bath and begin to see the results of my long and tedious work emerge on its surface. If I am lucky, a perfectly beautiful and original pattern will appear. I am very privileged to be able to do what I like most, developing my artistic talent while creating hand-made knives. My goal is to produce Mosaic Damascus steel that will be timeless in its appearance and artistic in its patterns and will also express my mood and inner feelings at the time of its creation.

Opposite, from the top:
"Four Hunting Knives", 2000-2002
All four blades have Explosion Damascus edges.
Mosaic Damascus blade and bolster, wild-boar tusk handle.
Overall length 9 3/4" (248 mm).
Mosaic Damascus blade and bolster, reindeer-horn handle.
Overall length 8 1/2" (216 mm).
Accordion Mosaic Damascus blade with Mosaic Damascus bolster, reindeer-horn handle.
Overall length 9 1/4" (235 mm).
Accordion Mosaic Damascus blade with Mosaic Damascus bolster, wild-boar tusk handle.
Overall length 10 1/4" (260 mm).

Left, from the top:

Creating a Mosaic Damascus Blade

1 Surface ground slices from pre-forged bars of Damascus steel are measured accurately and arranged to fit in the final design for the Mosaic blank. Thin bits of sheet nickel are cut, to be inserted between the Damascus pieces.

2 After all 69 pieces are set in their final arrangement, they are held together firmly by welding the corners of the Damascus blank.

3 The blank is now forge-welded and then forged close to the blade's final shape. It is important to forge very carefully so as not to distort the delicate patterns.

4 The blade is ground to shape then surface ground to reveal the patterns in the steel. Heat-treating and acid-etching bring out the final colors of the finished blade.

Opposite:

"Flowers", 2004

The 10 1/2" (267 mm) Flower Mosaic Damascus blade was created by combining slices of Mosaic steel made in 1997 and 2004. Explosion pattern Damascus edge and back. Bolsters are Mosaic Damascus, handle is fossil walrus ivory. Conny has made only 7 similar blades (with several rows of Mosaic Damascus) since 1997.

Overall length 15 5/16" (388 mm).

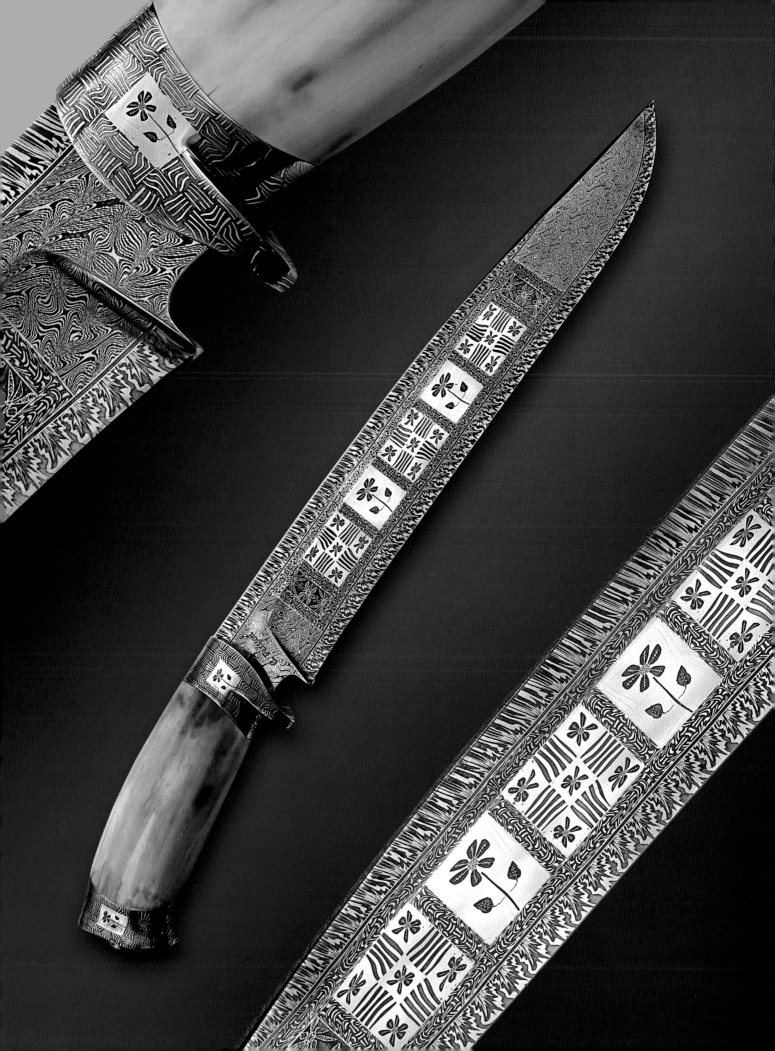

Above, from the top:

"Fighter", 1998
Twisted Damascus in the middle section of the blade with Twisted
Mosaic Damascus on each side and Explosion pattern Damascus along
the edges. Bolsters from Mosaic Damascus. Fossil walrus ivory handle.
Overall length 12 1/2" (318 mm).

"Hunting knife", 1998
Accordion Mosaic Damascus with Explosion pattern Damascus edge.
Mosaic Damascus bolster and willow root handle.
Overall length 8 1/2" (216 mm).

"Small hunting Knife", 1997
Mosaic Damascus blade with Explosion pattern Damascus edge (see
also enlargement at the top), Mosaic Damascus bolster and willow root
handle. Overall length 7 1/2" (190 mm).

Opposite, from the top:

"Flower Damascus Bowie", 1999
Mosaic Damascus blade with
Explosion pattern Damascus edge
and back. Mosaic Damascus bolster
and fossil walrus ivory handle. Best
Damascus Design award at the 1999
Atlanta Blade Show.
Overall length 15" (381 mm).

"Devil Damascus Bowie", 2002
Mosaic Damascus with Explosion
pattern Damascus edge and back,
Mosaic Damascus bolster. Fossil
walrus ivory handle. Best Damascus
Design award at the 2002 Atlanta
Blade Show as well as Best
Handmade Damascus award.
Overall length 16" (406 mm).

Above, from the right:
"Star Hunter", 2004
Mosaic Damascus blade with Explosion pattern Damascus edge and back, Mosaic Damascus bolsters. Handle made of dyed masur birch, silver spacers and a piece of fossil walrus ivory in the middle.
Overall length 9" (228 mm).

"Boar Hunter", 2004
Mosaic Damascus blade with Explosion pattern Damascus edge and back, Mosaic Damascus bolsters. Wild-boar tusk handle.
Overall length 8 3/4" (222 mm).

Opposite, from the top:
"Five Damascus Knives", 2004
All five knives with Explosion pattern Damascus edge and back.
Mosaic Damascus blade and bolster and fossil walrus ivory handle. Overall length 10" (254 mm).
Colored Mosaic Damascus blade, Mosaic Damascus bolster and wild-boar tusk handle.
Overall length 9" (228 mm).
Mosaic Damascus blade and bolster and dyed reindeer-horn handle.
Overall length 8 1/2" (216 mm).
Mosaic Damascus blade and bolster. Dyed masur birch handle with silver spacers and a piece of wild-boar tusk in the middle.
Overall length 9" (228 mm).
Mosaic Damascus blade and bolster and reindeer-horn handle.
Overall length 9" (228 mm).

Pierre Reverdy
Romans, France

Pierre Reverdy was born in 1960, in Saint Germain du Bois, France. In 1974, at the age of 14, he met his destiny at a handicraft fair when watching a blacksmith at work. This fascination has never left him since. On the contrary, it encouraged him to become one of the most talented contemporary bladesmiths, whose reputation is known internationally and recognized by numerous awards. When Pierre discovered his passion, he went to a technical school for 3 years and then for a 7-year training in metal forging at the Compagnons du Devoir.

After working in a forge in England and for some time with Daryl Meier in the USA, he returned to Paris, where he taught the use of metals for two years in the National School of Design. In 1989, with his wife, Nicole, he decided to become a professional knifemaker. Pierre eventually found his calling in forging Damascus steel, developing the traditional forging process to create his own trademark, le Damas Poétique, Poetic Steel. Instead of patterns appearing at random on the blade, he concentrated his efforts on producing blades showing deliberate patterns and images. Since 1991, he has created "a new way in steel". Every single blade is inspired by a theme chosen either by Pierre and Nicole or by a client, hence the notion "Poetic Steel". The motifs and the design of the knife tell a specific story, they reflect the soul of the knife and the artist who created it, making it a unique piece of art.

In November 2004, Pierre Reverdy had the honor to be awarded the very rare title of "Maitre d'Art", officially bestowed by the Minister of Culture. This honor is equal of the Cultural Treasure honors bestowed on artists in Japan. Pierre and Nicole succeed in realizing dreams in every art piece that leaves their studio. Every knife reflects the skills and the sensitivity of these talented artists and the memory of the fire from which it originated. The Reverdys have also produced two art books and are completing the third.

It's like a dream. Sometimes the collector dreams with me. Sometimes Nicole dreams with me about the creation of a knife. At first there is always reflection around a theme or an idea. Then come the sketches, many sketches, to create the vision, the right curves, the positive feeling, the pattern, the overall perfection... A three dimensional study on paper. Now the knife is ready to be fabricated, and it comes alive in the hands of its creator as the real magic begins: the evolution of the steel and the actual visual balance of an art piece, unfolding step by step. This makes me feel good. One idea pushes another, always with original solutions. It's a great adventure. The true essence of ART, that is what this is all about.

Opposite:
"Volute", 2001
Volute was inspired by generic forms, strong but smooth, shapes based on classic structures found in nature. Creating this special Poetic Damascus began with edm machine-cut basic blocks that were forged and reduced, then sliced and re-forged many times to create the unique patterns in the blade.
The guard was sculpted from one piece of steel. The handle is fossil walrus ivory decorated on the pommel with enamel on silver by Nicole Reverdy-Piel.
Overall length 12 9/16" (320 mm).

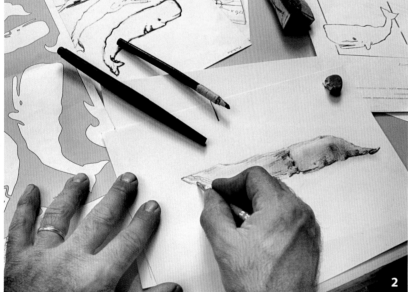

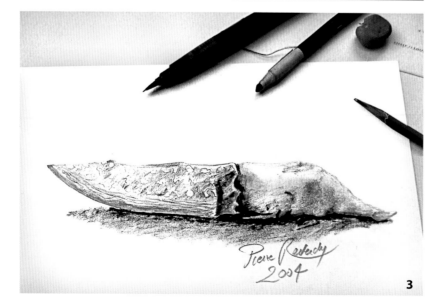

On the left:

Drawing the Design for "A Big Splash"

1 After deciding on the theme for the knife and its Poetic Damascus and making various sketches of its main subject, the Sperm Whale, Pierre begins to design the piece.

2 Slowly he gets down to the finer details, accurately incorporating his artistic concept in his drawing to create a new, one-of-a-kind art knife.

3 The drawing is finished and it is time to begin the actual construction process.

Opposite, pictures 1-8

"A Big Splash", 2004

For this knife Pierre chose the theme of Sperm Whales and water. The Sperm Whale is the sculpted handle, made from a fossilized walrus jaw bone. It is diving into the ocean, creating the waves on the top edge of the blade. In the Poetic Damascus motif, the whales can be seen jumping in and out of the water, playing together - all "frozen" in steel. Overall length 9" (228 mm).

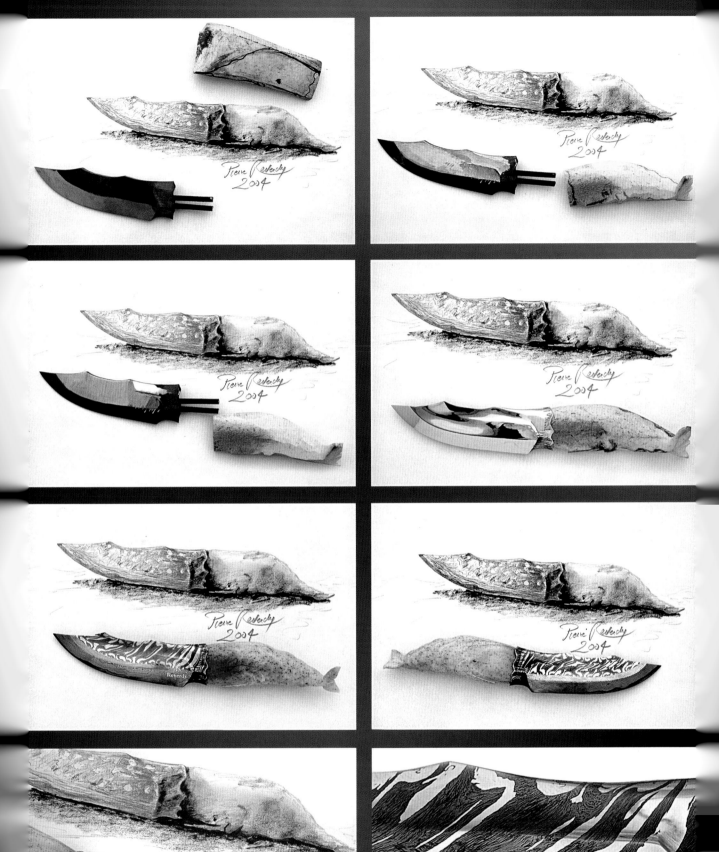

On the left:
"Brocatelle", 2001
The Reverdys are unique in the world of Damascus steel makers in that they do all the work in-house. From the programing and the cutting of the blocks through the complete forging process, carving and embellishments. They have also created the biggest collection in the world of cut patterns for creating their Poetic Damascus.

The Poetic Damascus for this knife was inspired by the design on a well known silky tissue made by "Le Manach", reflecting Louis XIII-style gate ironwork. The blade is carved like the folded tissue tied with a knot near the handle. The mammoth ivory handle is fully carved, and the wooden sheath is wrapped in Poetic Damascus and covered with rayskin. Overall length 14 1/6" (360 mm).

Opposite:
"Unicorn Dagger", 2003
Made of Poetic Damascus featuring unicorns and winged stags flying in from outer space. The handle, made by Nicole Reverdy-Piel, is enamel on Sterling silver with gold pins, showing the image of a unicorn on one side and that of a winged stag on the other. Rayskin-covered wooden sheath with Damascus fittings, enamel and gold pins. Overall length 11 13/16" (300 mm).

"Carreau D'argent", 2004
Forged from a new steel created by Pierre Reverdy, these
three knives are a sandwich of stainless steel and carbon
steel, with powdered metallurgic steel (2.2% carbon content)
for the cutting edge. Boxed as a set.
Overall length 7 7/8" (200 mm).

Opposite:
"Patrick's Dagger", 2001
Made as a gift from all his friends for
Patrick Louis Vuitton's 50th birthday,
the theme chosen for the Mosaic
Damascus was the hunting of a wild
boar. The basic blocks for creating
the chosen Poetic Damascus (seen
on the left) are the boar and 4 fox
terriers chasing it. The end result
makes up both edges of the dagger,
and the blade has a middle section of
50-layer Damascus steel representing
Patrick's 50 years of age.
Overall length 20 7/8" (530 mm).

Scott Slobodian
California, USA

Scott Slobodian was born in Philadelphia, Pennsylvania. After high school, he went into the military. It was there he made his first knife from an old bayonet. He also learned lapidary, ceramics and jewelry casting. Woodworking came with the family lumber business. His mother is a well known watercolor painter. Scott went to Penn State University and Oklahoma University, and then graduated with High Honors from the Art Center College of Design in Pasadena, California. He went on to become a successful commercial photographer and built a studio in Hollywood. During a shooting at a ceramics factory, Scott befriended the late Bob Engnath. Bob was the manager of the plant, but he also had a side business making and selling knife blanks to the muzzle-loading industry. In the early 80s, Bob began experimenting with the idea of recreating a decent samurai sword out of modern materials. Scott was fascinated and built several of Bob's blades. Then he bought his first Burr King grinder and started making Japanese blades himself, building on Bob's experiments and guidance. Joining the Guild in 1991 exposed him to Louis Mills and Jim Kelso, who made many masterpieces together. Scott felt he had found his path to artistic expression. In the late 90s, Scott won the coveted Knives Illustrated Art Knife of the Year Award four years in a row. He is a frequent winner of knife awards, is published worldwide and has knives in over 20 countries. In the mid-90s, Scott closed his studio, and he and his wife, Barbara, moved to Northern California and built a ranch with a large studio. The mountains look and feel like Japan, and the remoteness lends itself to the concentration needed for making fine swords. Most of Scott's knives are in the Japanese style; however he is known for his fantasy pieces, Bowies, and miniatures. This is something he does to keep fresh. Barbara brings her East Asian Studies degree to the family business by way of knowledge, inspiration and critique - and now her engraving. He continues to improve his product with new ideas, materials, and research.

Many years ago, a Japanese-American friend took me to see his family's old and treasured samurai sword. After committing every breach of sword-viewing etiquette and running my fingers all over the blade, I wanted to know why an old sword commanded so much reverence and respect. Later, armed with a little knowledge, I became enchanted. About this time, my wife received her East Asian Studies degree. She studied in Japan. The Shogun exhibit was also touring the country. I was primed. Musashi, who was Japan's greatest swordsman, was also a great painter, poet, writer, and ceramist. My love of making things, from models of cars, planes and boats, jewelry, furniture, guns and sculpture coalesced into the Samurai Sword. I truly value the blending of old steel technology, fish skins, rare woods, silk and fine jewelry into a cohesive work of art, the Japanese Sword.

Scott Slobodian

Opposite, from the left:
Fully Mounted Dress Tantos
"Summer", 1990

Tanto with an 11" (280 mm) clay-tempered 1050 steel blade. The mountings are silver and have been gold plated on the highlights and darkened in the shadows. The *saya* or sheath is a spectacular piece of dyed quilted maple with horn fittings and an original silk *sageo* (tie-down). The handle, or *tsuka*, is silk wrapped over manta ray skin.
Overall length 16" (406 mm).

"Storm", 1994

This Tanto has an 11" (280 mm) clay-tempered 1050 steel blade. All the fittings are iron and have a dragon theme. The silver *menuki* is also a dragon. The handle is wrapped with silk over fine rayskin.
Overall length 16" (406 mm).

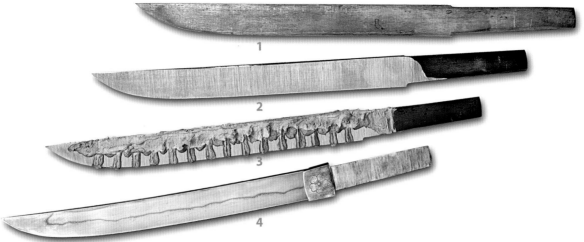

Making a War Tanto

1 The raw bar of 1050 steel is profiled.

2 The profiled blade is panel ground leaving the tang square.

3 The clay is applied to the roughed-out blade. It is now ready for heat treating.

4 The finished blade, clay-tempered, polished and with the finished *habaki* sleeve.

5 Clay-tempering: Scott is removing the heated blade prior to quenching. The kiln is 1500° Fahrenheit.

6 Wax Carvings: These are the carved wax fittings spruced up in preparation for casting.

7 Silver Castings: The wax is burned out and replaced by Sterling silver ready for fitting and engraving.

8 Engraving: Barbara Slobodian at her engraving station decorating the *tsuba* and handle fittings.

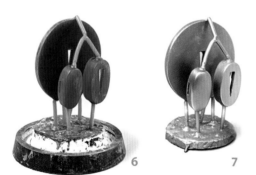

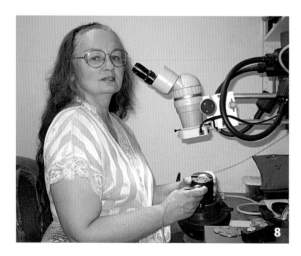

Opposite:

"Early Spring", 2004

This is a classical war Tanto. 500 years ago it would have been worn in the *obi* (belt) and tied down. It is in festival fittings. The blade is 11" (280 mm) long and is clay-tempered 1050 carbon-steel. It is hand polished to bring out the temper line. The Cherry Blossom Festival fittings are original and cast by Scott and engraved by Barbara Slobodian. The sheath or *saya*, is made of mazer birch which is dyed. The handle (*tsuka*) is leather wrapped over rayskin. The little *menuki* are cherry blossoms. The flared sheath is very typical of fancy sheaths of that era. The war Tanto is the equivalent of a big Bowie knife in weight and usage.

Opposite, from the left:

"Moon Dragon", 1999

The 14" (356 mm) blade, made of Turkish Twisted Damascus steel by Daryl Meier is hollow ground and flat ground. It has a silver moon and pure gold twin rings at the back of the blade. The handle was carved in Thailand from stag horn and commissioned through a broker. The furrel that holds it all together is silver that was casted by Scott. Overall length 20" (508 mm).

"Klingon", 1993

"I wanted to win the Knives Illustrated Art Knife of the Year Award. So, I spent an entire year building a knife-and-gun cased set in a fantasy realization of a "Ja-juk" set, a coming-of-age Klingon present. The object was to create a very otherworldly knife".

The blade is 8" (203 mm) and is re-forged Ferguson steel with a very thick 1095 core. The fittings are sculpted silver with pure gold Klingon letters on the guard. A carved Klingon skull forms the pommel and a gold necklace with a ruby at its throat. There are amalite stones set in gold bezels on the guard. The handle is made of spalted and dyed maple. The blade has been heavily etched, and the nickel has been solution-plated with copper to get a multicolored steel of brown, copper and silver.

"It eventually won the contest in 1993 and was featured in the magazine. Both of the knives shown here represent some of my best fantasy work, and both were a fun divergence from my Japanese work and its strict disciplines".

Overall length 13" (330 mm).

Above:

The "Patriarch of Petra", 1994

The blade is 9" (228 mm) long and made of re-forged Ferguson steel. The fittings are silver with 24k gold accents and a very large topaz stone in the pommel. The Arabian vine design was engraved by the late Peter Frankson. The wooden handle is spalted maple.

"I did not copy an existing design or idea, I just built it with the flavor of the Middle East. Petra has always been a fantasy place I would like to go to and it made a great concept for this knife. It's very blade-heavy and the forging "bark" has been left on the sides of the steel while the grinding revealed the layers. It was sold to a sultan in Abu Dubai. The silver guard and hilt were created in wax and appear to be floating. The mounts are hidden behind".

Overall length 14" (356 mm).

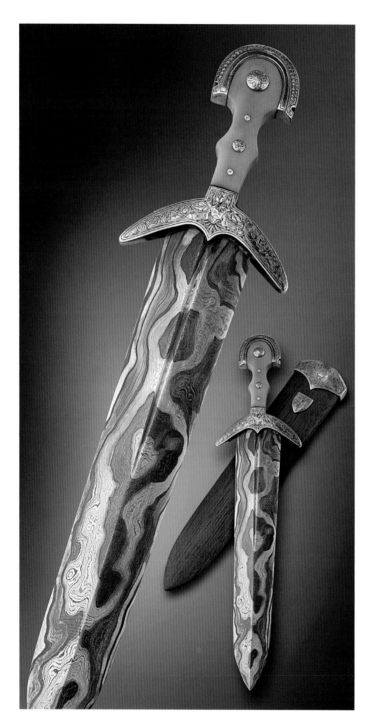

On the left:

"Cinquedea di da Vinci", 1994

This is a miniature with a blade only 3 1/2" (89 mm) long . Scott took a piece of Jim Feguson's Damascus and forged it into a miniature. It broke up the layers into interesting shapes and has been patinated to show colors in the various layers. The guard and pommel are pure gold and the handle fossil ivory. The sheath is fine grained bloodwood. The late Peter Frankson did the very tiny engraving, reflecting work from an original. The knife and sheath are displayed in a handsome box. Overall length 4 1/2" (114 mm).

Opposite, from the left:

Five "Kweiken" Tantos

These five knives represent the many looks of the *kweiken*, a small self-protection knife usually worn hidden in the *obi* belt or the sleeve of the kimono. It is the smallest of the samurai swords with the Tanto classification.

"Passion", 2002

This silver-mounted *kweiken* has a 4 1/2" (114 mm) blade made of clay-tempered 1050 steel. The wood is dyed and stabilized tiger maple. The *menuki* (the small handle sculpture) is a mandolin with a snake wrapped around it. Overall length 8 1/2" (216 mm).

"Destiny", 2003

The blade is 6 1/2" (165 mm), clay-tempered 1050 steel and is mounted in curly koa wood with copper fittings. *"I wanted a dark, moody knife".* It has a floral *menuki*. Overall length 10 1/2" (267 mm).

"Melange the Cat", 2002

The blade is 7 1/2" (190 mm) and is mounted in dyed and stabilized buckeye, a rare California root burl. The blade is clay-tempered 1050 steel, ground with a *Shino-ji*, which is a secondary grind that lightens a heavy blade. *"I had a wonderful time making this knife for an Italian friend in homage to his cat. The Chinese gold fittings made this a very colorful knife".* Overall length 11 1/2" (292 mm).

"Grass", 2003

The 6 1/2" (165 mm) blade, made of 1050 clay-tempered steel has a *Shino-ji* ground. It is mounted in buckeye but finished with silver fittings and horse *menuki*. Overall length 10 1/2" (267 mm).

"Pride", 2002

This silver-mounted kweiken has a 6" (152 mm) clay-tempered blade of 1050 steel, with a *Shino-ji* grind. The wood is Amboyna burl from Thailand. The *menuki* are floral. Overall length 10" (254 mm).

Dwight Towell
Idaho, USA

Dwight Towell was born in Midvale, Idaho, in 1934. He has continued to live at Midvale on a ranch that he owns and operates. His ranch is 3/4 of a mile from the homestead his great-grandfather settled in 1881 when he came to Idaho by wagon train from Missouri. Raised in a family that played musical instruments, Dwight now sings and plays mandolin in a bluegrass band. His family is very important to him. He met his future wife in high school, and for over fifty years she has been his helper. They raised a son and three daughters.

Dwight grew up hunting, fishing and using knives. He became interested in hand-made knives in the 1960s when he started seeing articles about hand-made knives and some of the makers. In 1966 he decided to try making a knife for his son as a Christmas present. He ground that knife on a hard wheel and hand-finished it. Having enjoyed making it, he continued to work on others. In 1970 he began seriously making knives, selling some locally. In 1972 he visited knifemaker Ted Dowell at Bend, Oregon. Ted encouraged him to join the Knifemakers' Guild, and in 1973 Dwight was accepted into the Guild, remaining actively associated with it ever since.

At first he was mainly making hunting and other using knives. Later he started making a few folding knives. One of his customers encouraged him to make some fancier knives, and this soon developed into one-of-a-kind art knives which in turn led him to decide to learn engraving. Encouraged by videos made by the engraver, the late Lynton McKenzie, Dwight now greatly enjoys engraving and working with raised gold and inlays.

The Art Knife Invitational Show was held in 1983 and 1984 in Reno, Nevada, and Dwight was invited to take part in that show both years. He was included in this prestigious group of makers and still actively makes knives for this event, held every other year in San Diego. Dwight has received many awards for his art knives, among them the Beretta Award in 1987 and the W. W. Cronk Memorial Award at the Knifemakers' Guild Show in 2002.

I feel very fortunate to have joined the group of custom knifemakers in the early 1970s. It has been a great time to be in a business that has grown and developed like it has. It has also been very exciting to watch developments in the craftsmanship and design.

The enjoyment and the friendships I have experienced over the years with fellow knifemakers and my customers is a source of great satisfaction. Knifemaking is very important to me. I always strive for the best knife I can make, with balance, flow of design, engraving and gold inlays compatible with the whole knife for overall eye appeal.

Dwight L. Towell

Opposite, from the left:
"Spanish Style Dagger", 2001
Made of Ladder pattern Damascus by Devin Thomas, the blade is 5 7/8" (149 mm) long and inlaid with 24k gold. Engraved bolsters and butt cap with 24k gold borders. Fossilized walrus ivory handle, with 24k gold beading inlay.
Overall length 10 7/8" (276 mm).
"Mediterranean Style Bowie", 1999
Made of Turkish Damascus by Jerry Rados. The 9" (228 mm) blade and blued steel handle are engraved and trimmed with 24k gold inlay by Dwight L. Towell. Overall length 14" (355 mm). This knife won the W.W. Cronk Memorial Award at the Knifemakers' Guild Show in Orlando, Florida, in July 2002.

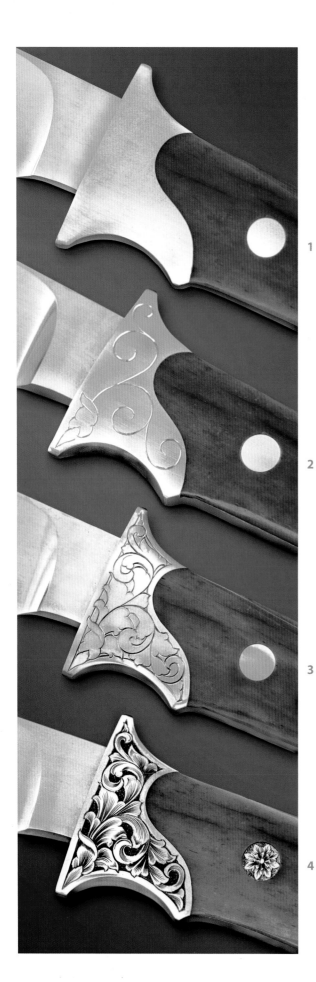

On the left:
Creating the Engraved Bolster
Dwight is well known for the crisp lines in his blades, his hand-sanded finish, and his hand-fitted bolsters, all accomplished by hands-on technique. He uses natural materials for his handles as much as possible, using woods, antlers, bone, sea shells, fossilized walrus or mammoth ivory. He has learned to make Damascus, but sometimes uses other makers' specialty Damascus for his blades.

"I showed the sequence photos of my engraving to portray how much the custom knife lends itself to embellishment, so that a person not acquainted with engraving can see the different steps taken and how much each phase of the engraving adds to the finished design".

1 Bare bolster made of 416 stainless steel.
2 The basic scroll lines cut into the steel.
3 The leaves added to the scrolls filling out the pattern.
4 Relieving and stippling the background and shading the leaves adds depth and dimension, and sculpts the pattern.
5 The tools used for the engraving (from the left): Pencil and scriber to sketch the design and then transfer it to the bolster; dividers used to lay out the border lines; flat graver for relieving the background. 90° square graver for cutting finer lines and shading; 120° square graver for cutting the pattern; pointed graver for stippling the background.

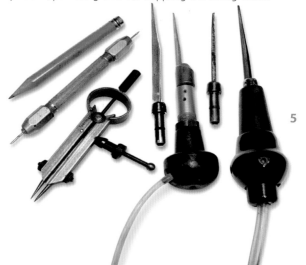

Opposite:
"Persian Style Knife", 2004
Giraffe bone handle and engraved stainless steel bolster enhance the Persian Style Knife with its 5 1/2" (140 mm) blade. The craftsmanship of the handmade knife and the artistry of engraving blend together to create a unique object of art in steel.
Overall length 10" (254 mm).

On the left:

"Dagger", 1989
Sole authorship dagger, made of
Cable Damascus. Blued-steel guard,
collar and butt cap with stainless
steel spacers. Handle made of fluted
Brazilian rosewood with Sterling
silver twisted wire inlay.
Blade length 5" (127 mm).

"Dagger", 1999
Sole authorship dagger made of
Damascus steel. Handle made of
charoite stone. Engraved guard and
butt cap with 24k gold borders.
Blade length 9 1/2" (241 mm).

"Dagger", 1999
Dark green marble handle having
French gray finished engraved guard
and butt cap with 24k gold borders.
24k raised gold inlays in collar and
butt cap. Sole authorship.
Blade length 7 1/2" (190 mm).

Opposite, from the left:

"Interframe Push-Dagger", 1987
Sole authorship push-dagger with
African blackwood inlay in the
handle and in the blade and 22k gold
wire inlay in the blackwood.
Blade length 4 3/16" (106 mm).

"Interframe Push-Dagger", 1993
African blackwood inlay in the
handle and in the blade, with 22k
gold wire and Mother-of-Pearl inlays
in the blackwood. Sole authorship.
Blade length 4 1/2" (114 mm).

Above, from the top:

"Full Tang Hunter", 1993
Curved bolster and flat ground 3 3/16" (81 mm) blade file-worked along its back. African blackwood handle with 22k gold and Mother-of-Pearl inlays. Sole authorship.

Full Tang Hunter", 1985
Dahl Sheep-horn full tang hunter with 4" (101 mm) blade.

"Hidden Tang Knife", 1984
Spiral fluted elephant ivory handle with Sterling silver twisted wire in grooves. File work trim on the fittings. Oval ivory inlay in the butt cup. Sole authorship. Blade length 4 1/4" (108 mm).

Opposite, from the left:

"Mediterranean Style Dirk", 1983
Snakewood handle with twisted Sterling silver wire inlay. Sole authorship.
Blade length 10 1/2" (267 mm).
Overall length 16 3/4" (425 mm).

"Searles Style Bowie", 1984
Snakewood handle with twisted Sterling silver wire inlay. Filework on fittings. Sole authorship.
Blade length 9 1/4" (235 mm).
Overall length 14 1/4" (362 mm).

"Mediterranean Style Bowie", 1995
Fossilized mastodon ivory handle. Engraved bolster, top and end of tang with 24k gold borders. Sole authorship.
Blade length 7 3/8" (187 mm).
Overall length 12 1/4" (311 mm).

Buster Warenski
Utah, USA

Buster Warenski was born in 1942, in Kimberly, Nevada. Fortunate to live in prime hunting and fishing country, and being one who enjoys working with his hands, in 1966 he began making hunting knives as a hobby. It was quite apparent early on that this young man had talent. Word spread quickly in the fledgling Utah knife community, and this led to an opportunity in the spring of 1972 for Buster to work briefly in the custom shop of the late Harvey Draper (Draper Knives), one of the world's first custom makers. In this atmosphere, Buster was able to quickly and precisely fine-tune his skills. After working with Draper for six months, Buster returned to his hometown of Richfield, Utah, and began making knives full-time. Rather than hunters and skinners, most of his production was high-end art knives, many embellished with his own engraving and gold inlay. Early in his knifemaking career he also taught engraving. In fact, his lovely wife, Julie, attended his engraving classes (prior to their marrying) and now works side-by-side with him, embellishing both Buster's knives and those of other knifemakers. In 1973 Buster joined the Knifemakers Guild, and by 1984 he had served nine years on the board of directors, two terms as president, and also in the positions of vice president and director. Naturally, he is a regular at all the Guild Shows, and he attends a few other major venues each year, including the biennial Art Knife Invitational Show in San Diego, California. The art knives this gentleman creates are very unique, they're all one-of-a-kind, and they're simply beautiful.

Today, after 18 years of marriage, Buster states *"We are still enjoying the romance of a beautiful marriage and we're a very successful knifemaking team. We can't ask for anything more".* Not a smith, Buster buys Damascus and standard steel bar stock, as do many makers, and performs all other operations involved in creating art knives in his well-equipped shop. He is the sole author of all his knives, although Julie does embellish most of them with engraving and gold inlay art.

Warenski Knives has been enjoying a great success as a business since 1973. The rewards have been great, allowing us to make a living doing something we love. Entering knifemaking as a vocation, I was able to lead a comfortable life as well as take an active part in the early years of the Knifemakers Guild. We have seen the growth of this industry from a handful of collectors to a worldwide movement, elevating contemporary knives to an accepted art form. Julie and I have dedicated ourselves to absolute excellence in our knives and engraving.

Opposite:
"Fire and Ice", 1995
This, the third knife in Warenski's Legacy Series, was designed with rubies and diamonds, hence its name, "Fire and Ice". The 8" (203 mm) blade is made of work-hardened 18k gold. The handle is rutilated quartz crystal with light reflecting golden rutile crystals. All the fittings and the sheath are 18k gold sculpted and engraved. In all, 28 ounces of 18k gold, 22 rubies (4.25 carats) and 75 diamonds (7 carats). The red gouache-type enameling adds the final "blaze" to the "fire". Engraving by Julie Warenski.
Overall length 13" (330 mm).

On the left:

Making the Agate Dagger

Buster Warenski is seen here working on the various parts that make up this dagger.

1 Filing the guard to shape from a bar of nickel-silver.

2 Shaping the agate handle.

3-4 grinding the 440C stainless steel blade.

5 finishing the the nickel-silver sheath.

When Buster is done, everything goes on to his wife, Julie, for engraving, gold inlay and stone setting.

Opposite:

"Agate Dagger", 2004

The 440C stainless steel blade is 7" (178 mm) long, the handle is made of agate and the fittings and sheath are nickel-silver. Button on sheath is topped with a topaz. Engraving and gold inlay by Julie Warenski.

Above:

"Crystal Push-Dagger", 2002

The 440C stainless steel blade is 5"
(127 mm) long, the handle is 416
stainless steel inset with a panel of
blued steel that has been engraved
and gold inlaid, then covered with
an inlay of optical grade quartz. The
sheath is nickel-silver with gold inlay
and engraving. Engraving and gold
inlays by Julie Warenski.
Overall length 7 1/2" (190 mm).

Opposite, from the left:

"Pietersite Dagger", 2000

A mid-sized dagger with a handle of pietersite rock from Africa and an
8 1/2" (216 mm) blade of 440C stainless steel. The fittings and sheath
are nickel-silver, engraved and gold inlaid by Julie Warenski.
Overall length 13 1/4" (336 mm).

"Ivory Dagger", 1998

A large dagger with carved ivory handle and a 10 1/2" (267 mm) 440C
steel blade. The carved ivory is accented with blued steel fittings.
Engraving and gold inlay by Julie.
Overall length 15 1/4" (387 mm).

"Jade Dagger", 1999

The spiraled dark green jade handle adds a touch of elegance to this
large dagger. A 10" (254 mm) 440C steel blade and blued steel fittings.
French-gray engraving and gold inlay by Julie complete this art knife.
Overall length 15 1/4" (387 mm).

"Letter Opener", 2001

With premium quality lapis lazuli handle, a 7 1/2" (190 mm) blade
of 440C steel and blued fittings with gold inlay, this letter opener
becomes a desk accessory for a very successful person.
Overall length 11 1/2" (292 mm).

Above:

"Ruby Tour de Force", 2003
Wasp-shaped 11 1/2" (292 mm)
blade, fashioned from 440C
stainless steel, is pierced and
sculpted. The handle, made from
a single ruby crystal, is inlaid
with a band of silver set with
rubies. The fittings are blued steel
with carved silver with blued
steel overlays. Carving and stone
setting by Julie Warenski.
Overall length 17 1/2" (445 mm).

opposite:

"King Tut Dagger", 1987
Buster Warenski's "King Tut Dagger" is a faithful solid gold reproduction
of the solid gold knife found with the 3,300-year-old mummy of the
Egyptian pharaoh Tutankhamen. This project, conceived in the early
1980s, helped spearhead the contemporary art knife renaissance. The
first knife in Warenski's Legacy Series, it is entirely made of 18k gold and
24k gold. _"After 4 years of experimenting and learning, I was able to
complete the project. Some of the difficult techniques used here were
granulation and cloisonne. Casting the blade was also a real challenge,
as it required pouring nearly 10 oz. of 18k gold. After several failures, I
was able to make the casting by first making a steel mold. This is by far
the most complicated project I have ever done"._
Overall length 12 1/2" (317 mm).
From the collection of Phil Lobred, USA.

Yoshindo Yoshihara
Tokyo, Japan

Yoshindo Yoshihara, born in 1943, is very proud of being the 10th generation in his family to work as a swordsmith or blacksmith. Until his grandfather, Kuniie, began to work as a swordsmith in 1933, the family tradition was in the fields of blacksmithing and toolmaking, although in Japan, toolmakers made their tools from the traditional Japanese steel called *tama hagane*, the same as swordsmiths. They would fold and forge their steel to produce an optimal material for their tools. Kuniie was the head of a very successful family of toolmakers, which extended back at least four or five generations. In the early 20th century the Japanese government made serious efforts to revive the production of traditional swords and to train large numbers of new swordsmiths. Part of this was the creation in 1933 of a school to teach these methods, a school Kuniie attended and would one day direct. Yoshindo's father, Masahiro, and great-uncle, Kuninobu, also were active swordsmiths. With the end of World War II, all weapon production came to a halt in Japan; but in 1953 the government allowed a group of swordsmiths to produce 300 swords, which were to be presented to the heads of state of countries belonging to the United Nations. Kuniie was active in this effort, and 10 year old Yoshindo helped in the shop and began learning the basics of swordmaking. The family had returned to making hand-forged tools after the war, but with great improvements in the Japanese economy by 1970, Yoshindo returned to being a full-time swordsmith. From early in his career, Yoshindo won many prizes in national sword competitions, and in 1983 he was declared *mukansa*, which means his work would thenceforth be displayed but not judged in the annual national sword competition. In March 2004, he was named an important living cultural asset of the City and Prefecture of Tokyo. His brother, Shoji, is also a swordsmith and *mukansa*, and his son, Yoshikazu, is now a *mukansa*-level swordsmith and works with his father.

The traditional craft of the Japanese sword has survived into the 21st century and is a viable art and craft today, but it still faces obstacles for its survival into the future. Ironically, the major problem faced by Japanese smiths now is the limit placed on the number of blades a smith may produce. This is a law written by the postwar Japanese government (called the Ju-To Ho law), which was intended to eliminate or limit weapon production in early post-WWII Japan. Hopefully this law will be modified or repealed in the 21st century, providing a great deal of support and help for traditional Japanese swordsmiths in Japan.

Opposite, from the left:
"Moroha Tanto", 2001
This double-edged style Tanto has a wide and very strong complex *hamon* on both edges.
Overall length 13 3/16" (350 mm).
From the collection of A. Compeau, USA.
"Hocho Masamune Tanto", 1986
A full size Tanto, made in the style of the famous 13th-century swordsmith Masamune, with traditional engravings (*horimono*) and grooves cut all the way through the blade.
Overall length 12 1/6" (311 mm).
"Katakiri-ha Tanto", 1998
This straight blade has a carving (*horimono*) of a stylized sword (*ken*) and a *gunome* pattern *hamon* or a series of regular semi-circles.
Overall length 10" (254 mm).

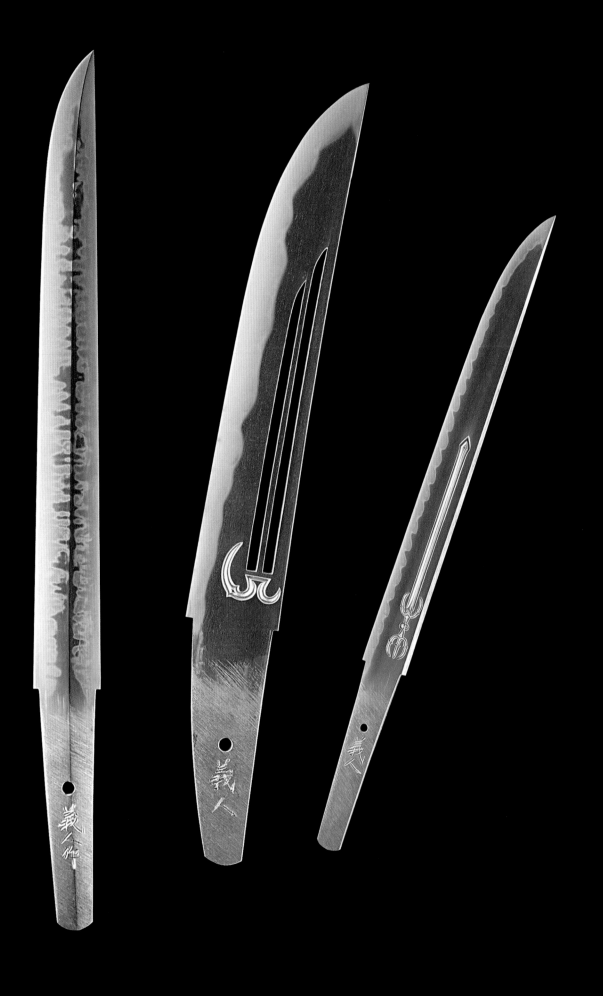

On the left:
Yoshindo at his forge (left) and making a blank, or sunobe, for a blade out of a bar of *tama hagane* (right).

Opposite, from the top left:
Making the Hira-Tsukuri Tanto, 2004
1 Tama hagane, the traditional starting material for a Japanese blade, is made from iron-ore mined in sand form and processed in a charcoal-fueled smelter in Japan.
2 Sunobe: The blank for the Tanto, forged out of a bar of steel made from the *tama hagane*, which has been folded over onto itself about 12 times.
3 Hizukuri: The *sunobe* is forged into a rough shape and the edge and point and other parts of the blade are now forged into the proper shape.
4 Namatogi: The blade is shaped with a file (on the edge and back) and sometimes with a drawknife on the sides and then filed into shape.
5 Tsuchioki: Clay is placed on the blade to make the hamon. Yoshindo uses a black clay for the body and edge, and then adds a second layer of red clay over this. The complex pattern of red clay strips near the edge will produce the proper *choji*-shaped *hamon* after heating and quenching the blade in water.
6 Kaji-togi: This refers to the rough polishing done by the smith after making the *hamon*, usually using a large grinding wheel that has a stream of water pouring over it in order to keep the blade cool. After using the grinding wheel and one or two additional polishing stones, the shape and edge of the blade are now well defined, and some features of the surface such as the *hamon* are now visible.
7 Yaki-ire: After using the grinding wheel and several more polishing stones, the *hamon* outline is now clearly visible.
8 Planning the **Horimono**: Yoshindo outlines the *hamon* in ink and then makes a preliminary sketch of the horimono on the blade. The *horimono* must not be designed near the *hamon* because the *hamon* steel is too hard to cut into.
9 Finishing the **Horimono** and **signing the Tang**: The *horimono* is finished using a series of small chisels and a hammer. The carvings are a series of Chinese characters showing a traditional Zen Buddhist expression meaning "the entire world is one". The tang is finished with decorative file marks and the signature is inscribed on the tang and written from the top to the bottom. It reads: *"kokaji Yoshindo hori do saku"* or "this blade and the *horimono* (carving) were both made by the swordsmith Yoshindo". After this it will go to a polisher for a final polish that will bring out all the details of the steel as well as the *hamon*, and produce the final refined shape of the blade.
10 Oshigata: An *oshigata* is a tracing of the entire blade. A piece of charcoal is then used to make a rubbing over this tracing to show the the details of the signature and the *horimono*. The *hamon* is drawn in by hand after the tracing and rubbing is done. An *oshigata* is the traditional method by which details of a Japanese blade are captured on paper for publication or record keeping. Details of the *hamon* and signature are usually better depicted in an *oshigata* than with a photograph. This traditional method of recording the details of a sword goes back over 400 years.
Overall length (including tang) 13 7/8" (352 mm).

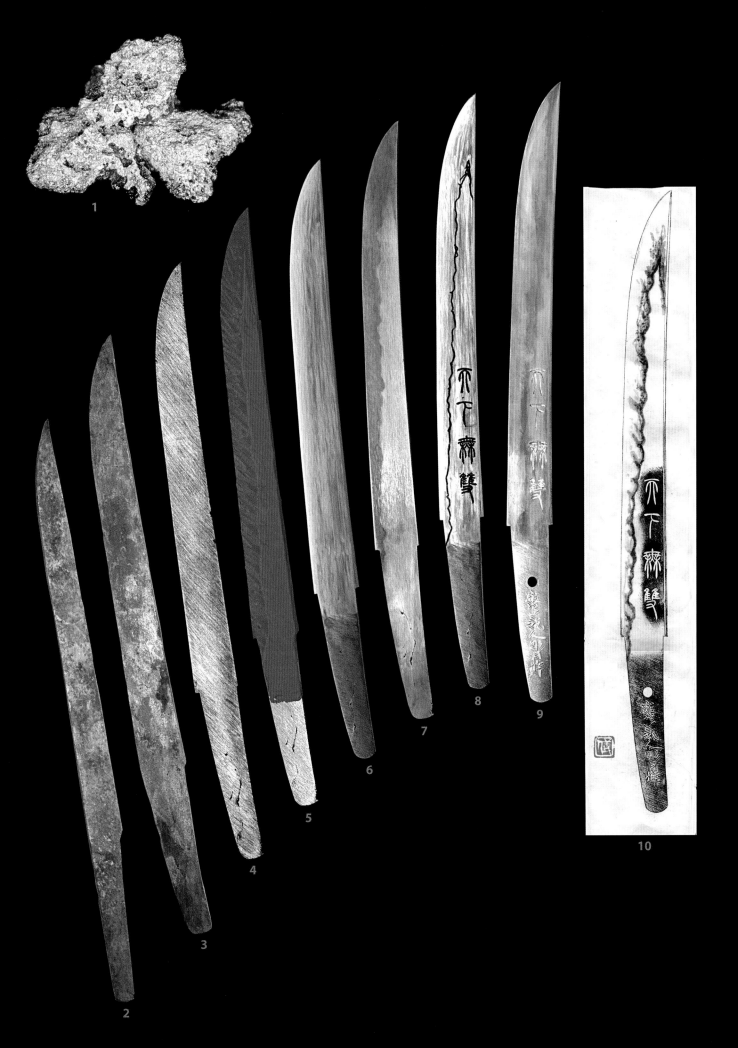

Appreciating a Japanese Blade

By Leon Kapp, USA

Before one can appreciate a Japanese sword, one must understand the basic differences between it and a Western knife. The methods of making and finishing the two types of blades are very different and, therefore, so are the ways of looking at, evaluating and appreciating the two types of work. After a swordsmith has made a Japanese blade, it is polished and then put into a simple white wood scabbard called a *shira-saya*, intended only to protect and store the blade but not designed to be a functional or practical mount. If the new owner wants a traditional, functional mount, he must then ask the swordsmith to have other craftsmen make one for his new blade, and he must decide how elaborate it should be and in what style it should be made. When looking at a Japanese blade, it is usually removed from its mount or *shira-saya*. An appraisal of an individual blade starts by looking at the *sugata* (shape), the *hamon* (the pattern of the heat-treated hardened edge), and the *jitetsu* or *jigane* (the surface texture and appearance of the steel with its visible surface pattern or grain called the *jihada*). The lines of a Japanese sword should be clean and well proportioned. The steel itself is the most important single element of the blade and usually has a distinct color and texture, and a pattern on the surface from the repeated folding of the steel.

The surface grain pattern is frequently very subtle and difficult to detect, its intensity or *jihada*, is determined by the swordsmith. The pattern of the hardened edge should be very clear and form an unbroken line, without gaps or discontinuities. In addition, the edge pattern, or *hamon*, should have a recognizable traditional shape. For a sword to be examined properly, the blade must have a good polish and be in good condition. The polishing is done using a series of water-lubricated natural stones; no chemicals are used, nor any type of etching process. Modern synthetic stones cannot bring out the essential details in the Japanese steel. This polishing process is a very old Japanese art and craft and may itself have a history of around 800 years.

Another unique difficulty in appreciating the Japanese sword is that it is very difficult to photograph. It is a challenge to capture the subtle details of the steel surface or the complexities of the *hamon*. A customary and traditional way of showing the details of a Japanese sword in print is to make an *oshigata* of the blade: The outline of the blade and the details of the tang and signature are captured on tracing paper, using charcoal, and the details of the *hamon* are then carefully drawn in by hand. Traditionally, swords shown in publications are presented with both a photograph and an *oshigata*, to show the details of the *hamon*.

Opposite:

Hira-Tsukuri Tanto and Oshigata, 2004
The detailed process of creating this special Tanto for the book is described on previous pages in this section.
Overall length (including tang) 13 7/8" (352 mm).

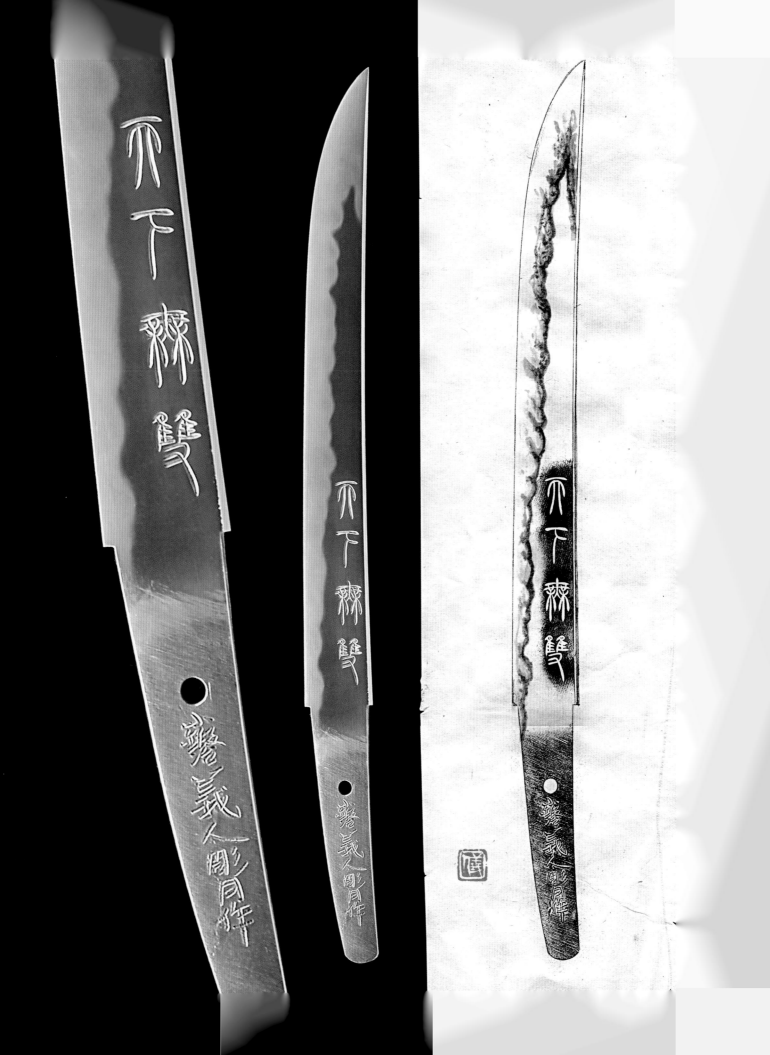

Above:

"Early Winter Tanto", 1993

This Tanto is unique in that it was commissioned by a Japanese collector as a traditionally forged blade by Yoshindo Yoshihara, to be mounted with a *koshirae* made by a non-Japanese, Jim Kelso. Jim chose to honor this choice by mounting it in a traditional style; he wished to keep the overall form simple, as befits the austere line of the blade. The motif is "Early Winter", with fallen leaves among snow and ice. Materials are ebony wood, gold, silver, copper and enamel. Overall length 16 6/8" (425 mm).

Opposite, from the left:

Miniature "Hocho Masamune Tanto", 1991

The blade's details and *horimono* (carving) are similar to those on the full-sized Tanto, but it's length is only 3 11/12" (93 mm). This is the only miniature ever made by Yoshindo to this scale. *From the collection of Dr. L. Marton, USA.*

"Tosu", 1996

A highly decorated utility knife used by Japanese noblemen in the 8th century. The carved and decorated fossil ivory scabbard was made by Yoshindo's daughter, Maiko, in the same style seen in 8th-century originals.
Overall length 3 7/16" (87 mm). *From the collection of Dr. L. Marton, USA.*

"Kozuka-Kogatana", 1999

This is a one-piece blade (*kogatana*) with *hamon* and hilt (*kozuka*). The decorative silver and copper inlay on the handle depicts a swordsmith's special tongs used to hold raw *tama hagane* at the beginning of the forging process.
Overall length 8 5/16" (222 mm).

"Kozuka-Kogatana", 2002

A blade (*kogatana*) with an integral hilt made from a single piece of *tama hagane*. The gold wire inlay is in a traditional pattern preserved at the 8th-century Shoso-in Temple in Nara, Japan. Overall length 9 1/2" (240 mm).

"Kaiken", 1990

A small Tanto usually worn by Samurai women in the Edo period (1600-1868). Yoshindo made a simple and smooth *koshirae* that would have been worn in the opening of a *kimono* or in an *obi* or sash. All lacquer with a gold *menuki* (handle ornament).
Overall length 10 3/4" (270 mm).

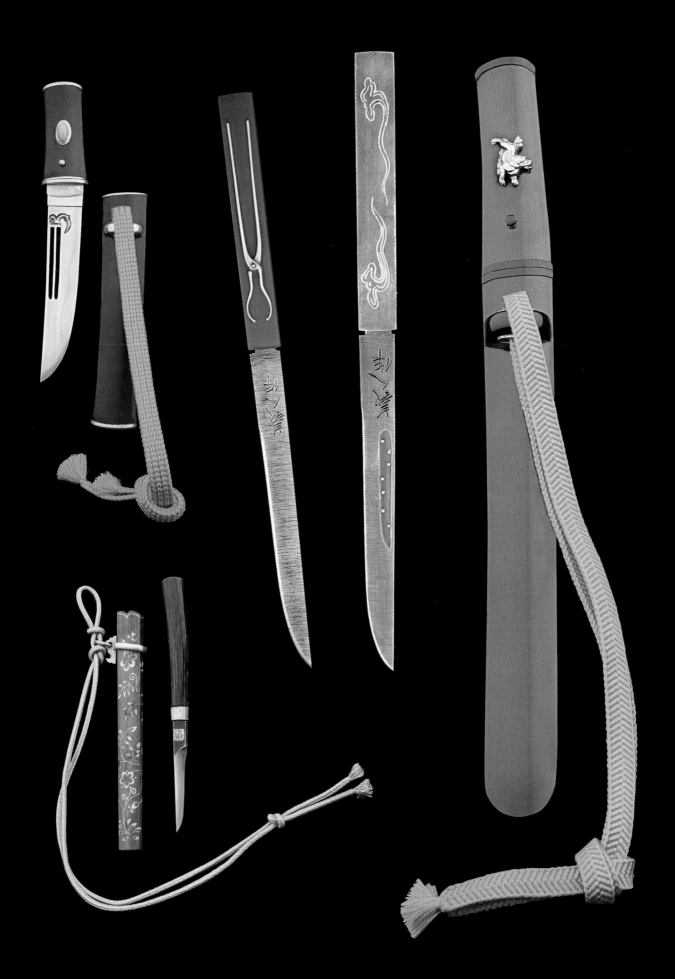

Epilogue

Fulfilling a dream once is something that warms one's heart for many years. I still find it hard to believe that I have done it twice. But, during these 18 intensive months of adding a new volume to the Custom Knife printed Hall of Fame, I was not alone. Enthusiastic encouragement came from all around the world. Hints and suggestions, sometimes from complete strangers, created in me a chain of ideas that enhanced many pages in this book.

The excitement created by rumors about this second book nourished me with renewed strength and enabled me to complete the obviously missing counterpart to what I had begun only two years earlier. And again, here too, the mission was nearly impossible. While enjoying the fruits of my first adventure, I had virtually forgotten just what was needed to get a selected group of artists from all over the world to cooperate with me and work as a team. I had nearly forgotten what it takes to get all of them doing "extra-curricular" work, sticking religiously to fixed timetables and deadlines from over 10,000 miles away.

These weren't easy months. Here too there were many moments of despair, frustration, endless hours of coaching, coaxing and encouraging, and a lot of patience in overcoming multitudinous setbacks, which, if listed here, would fill many pages. Luckily for all of us, there was also much love and faith involved, and that is what finally pulled it off.

The resulting joint achievement is again a printed exhibition of modern custom knife art, showing the world how talented men and women bring forth secrets hidden in steel and breathe life and great beauty into pieces of metal.

Maybe, when we get together again, 10 years from now (didn't I say this only two years ago?), when styles, materials and designs in custom knives are totally different, I might be tempted to do the "nearly impossible" all over again.

Creating the Illustrations

Some of the best photographers in the world took part in photographing the original knife images for this book. Here too, as in Art and Design in Modern Custom Folding knives, all of the original images were digitally manipulated, with their permission, to create the final illustrations.

Producing the illustration pages for this book demanded over 1,000 hours of exciting, creative computer work, using a 1.25 MH Mac G4 computer and Adobe Photoshop 8.0 CS imaging software.

Creating a relatively complicated full-page illustration for the book required, at times, great expertise. The following stages were involved in creating the sample shown opposite, which was used in the book for a full-page color illustration in Chantal Gilbert's section.

Below:
Combining two photographs
Two pictures, showing both sides of Gay Rocha's little knife (forged from a file), were combined to create this illustration for posting on the Internet. Photoshop 8.0 CS was used on a Macintosh G4 computer, with images shot hand-held with a tiny 4 MP Canon "IXUS-i" digital camera using available fluorescent room lighting. The whole process, including the digital photography, "removing" one knife from its background and "planting" it on the final picture, took less than 1 hour. This includes digitally "cleaning" the steel from unwanted reflections and color casts.

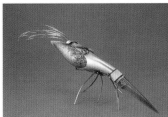

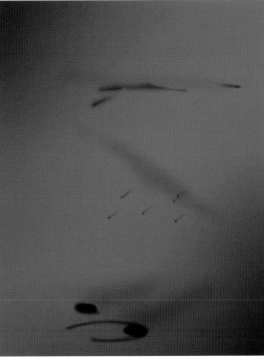

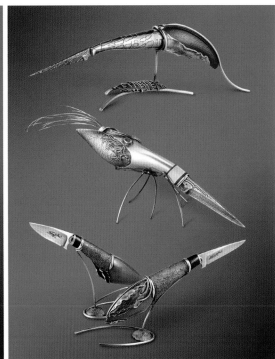

Above:

The Artistry of Nir Darom

An example of the subtleties required to create a full-page illustration for the book is demonstrated in this series of pictures. Three separate transparencies were chosen and scanned. The knife images were "removed" from their original backgrounds and a new background (blue) was created. After the knife images were carefully color-corrected and arranged on the new background, complex shadows were created (shown here with the knife layers "hidden" from view), giving the final illustration a "natural" look. See Chantal Gilbert's section for the full page illustration. This is the Photoshop artistry of Nir Darom.

1 Planning the final layout of the page.

2 Scanning 3 original transparencies.

3 Digitally "removing" the image of the knife from its original background (using Photoshop's "Pen Tool") to later place it on a newly created one.

4 Creating a color background that complements the knives to be placed on it; shading certain sections for a more dramatic effect.

5 Arranging the knife images on the newly created page as planned.

6 Removing undesired color reflections from the knife images and, color correcting the steel, gold, silver and various other elements on each knife.

7 Finally, creating the subtle shadows separately for each knife by combining small shadow elements built separately (in this case) on 12 different layers, giving the finished illustration a natural look.

All in all, 17 layers combined into one illustration - the background layer, corner shadings layer, 3 knife layers and 12 separate shadow layer sections - and about 4 hours with Nir Darom in front of the computer.

Photography

Eric Eggly, PointSeven Inc.
810 Seneca Street, Toledo,
OH 43608, USA
Phone: (419) 243-8880
email: eric@pointsevenstudios.com
Site: www.pointsevenstudios.com

Francesco Pachì
Via Pometta, 1
17046 SASSELLO (SV), Italy
Phone/Fax: (+39) 01 9720086
email: info@pachi-knives.com
Site: www.pachi-knives.com/homeita.htm

Jim Cooper, SharpByCoop.com
9 Mathew Court
Norwalk, CT 06851, USA
Phone: (203) 838-8939
email: coop747@optonline.net
jcooper@sharpbycoop.com
Site: http://www.sharpbycoop.com

Dr. Fred Carter, Mitchell Lum, Steve Towell, Tom Lansing, Dino
Petrocelli, Scott Slobodian, Jim Kelso, KnifeArt.com, Louise
Bilodeau, Larry Linkous, Michel Gauvint, Rob Nicoll, Marc Mesplié,
Alain Miville-Deschenes, Tom Kishida, Leon (Lonnie) Kapp, Jessica
Marcotte and Paolo Saviolo.

Gaetan Beauchamp

Born in 1957, in Canada, his knife art was influenced in by the vast woodland areas north of Quebec. The handles for his knives, crafted of various natural materials, are usually scrimshawed with wild life scenes.

From left to right:

"Cougar Head" Twin Set, 2004

Handles made of Water Buffalo horn and mammoth ivory, bolsters are 416 SS and the blade made of Devin Thomas stainless Damascus.

Overall length 9 1/4" (235 mm).

"Lion", 2004

Handle made of Water Buffalo horn, bolsters are 416 SS and the blade made of ATS-34.

Overall length 8 3/4" (222 mm).

"Leopard eyes", 2004

Handle made of Water Buffalo horn, bolsters are 416 SS and the blade made of ATS-34.

Overall length 9 3/4" (248 mm).

Contact Information

Contributors for the introduction

Dennis Greenbaum
2 Penny Lane
Baltimore, MD 21209, USA
Phone: (410) 960-1473
email: dgreenbaum@comcast.net

Born in Cleveland, Ohio, in 1951, Dennis is a marketing executive with over 30 years of experience working in radio, TV, and advertising agencies, Dennis has spent the past 20 years as a brand consultant specializing in graphic design and multimedia. Although not a graphic designer himself, Dennis has found that all those years working around high-end design apparently rubbed off and is evident in the work he's been doing as a custom knifemaker. When not at the office, most of his spare time is spent either in his well-equiped, home knife-workshop; or at his computer, where he can be found in any one of several knife forums, interacting with fellow makers and knife afficionados from all over the world.
Dennis and his lovely wife Michelle have been happily married since 1984. Michelle has been teaching High School Math for over 30 years. Their teenage daughter Piper is not only an Honor student, but is already demonstrating talents as a gifted musician.

Don Guild
email: don@guildknives.com
Site: http://www.guildknives.com

Born in 1927, a native of California, Don lives most of the year in Hawaii. His many years in the antique trade have influenced his knife collecting. He collaborates with knifemakers to develop classic motifs and themes, and delights in working with under-appreciated knifemakers, occasionally writing about his heroes.

Phil Lobred
email: hmmail@hmlanding.com
Site: http://www.sanfranciscoknives.com

Born in 1944 in Washington D.C., Phil currently lives in San Diego. Collects custom knives since 1968. In 1979 he began to focus on California (San Francisco) style knives, both contemporary and antique. Phil started the Art Knife Invitational Show in 1983.

Dr. Larry Marton
email: marton@cellgateinc.com

In partnership with his wife Marlene, Larry has been collecting knifes for about 20 years. Their collection focuses on knives that challenge the creativity of the maker, thus stimulating the expansion of the maker's artistry.

Deryk C. Munroe
P.O. Box 3454
Bozeman, MT 59772-3454, USA
Phone: (406) 585-2279
email: deryk@munroedesign.com
Site: http://www.dcmunroeknives.com

Born in 1973, Deryk has been making knives full time since 1998, specializing in one-of-a-kind concept creations, Damascus and high-tech utility folders. He lives in Montana with his wife, Jana, where they spend most of their free time exploring the woodlands of the Rocky Mountain Front.

Ricardo Velarde
7240 Greenfield Dr.
Park City, Utah 84098 USA
Phone: (801) 360-1413
email: ricardovelarde@velardeknives.com
Site: http://www.velardeknives.com

Born in Mexico City in 1957 and recruited by Brinham Young University after the Montreal Olimpics as a diver Ricardo moved to Utah, U.S.A. in 1977. Ricardo's business followed his first love, falconry, with a small workshop that produced equipment for the sport. As custom knives began to catch his interest he worked with S.R. Johnson and Dietmar Kressler who shared with him their vast knowledge. His "Forte" undoubtedly is the detail on his knives.

Ed Wormser, USA
Phone: (847) 757-9926
email: edw11@aol.com

An avid collector and recently a knife show promoter, currently promoting 2 yearly knife shows in the USA. The Chicago Custom Knife Show in September and the Las Vegas Tactical Invitational, in January.

Don Cowles, USA

Born in California in 1941, he currently resides in Royal Oak, Michigan. Don made his first knife in 1963 and now makes cutlery of his own design, mainly small straight knives to be carried like a fountain pen in a specially designed sheath. He has a well-equipped shop, but most of his effort expended in making a knife is hand work. Don is a member of the Miniature Knifemakers Society and contributes as a moderator to online knife discussion forums.

From the left:

"Gold Spear", 2004

Devin Thomas Raindrop pattern stainless Damascus. Bolsters are 416 stainless steel. Scales are Gold-Lip Mother of Pearl with 14k gold pins. Blade accents are also 14k gold. A topaz, set in 14k gold, is fitted in the ricasso. Overall length 5 3/4" (146 mm).

"Abalone Gent", 2004

Devin Thomas Raindrop pattern stainless Damascus. Bolsters are 416 stainless steel. Scales are abalone with 14k gold pins. Blade accents are also 14k gold. A ruby set in 14k gold is fitted in the ricasso. Overall length 5 1/2" (140 mm).

"Ivory Gent", 2001

Mirror polished RWL34 stainless; 416SS bolsters; 14k gold pins; fossil mammoth ivory scales with scrimshaw by Diane Hecht. Overall length 5 1/2" (140 mm).

Contact Information

Featured Artists

Van Barnett
168 Riverbend Blvd., St. Albans,
WV 25177, USA
Phone: (304) 727-5512
email: ArtKnife@charter.net
Site: www.vanbarnett.com

Charlie Bennica
Salet F-34190 Moulès et Baucels,
France
Phone/Fax: (+ 33) 4 67 73 4240
email: charly.bennica@club-internet.fr
Site: http://www.bennica-knives.com

Roger Bergh
Dalkarlsa 291, 91894 Bygdea,
Sweden
Phone: (+46) 93430061
Cell-phone: (+46) 705941574
email: roger@roger-bergh.nu
Site: http://www.roger-bergh.nu

Arpad Bojtos
Dobsinskeho 10, 984 03 Lucenec,
Slovakia
Phone: (+421) 47 4333512
email: bojtos@stonline.sk

David Broadwell
4726 Kmart Drive, Wichita Falls,
TX 76308, USA
Phone: (940) 692-1727
email: david@broadwell.com
Site: http://www.david.broadwell.com

Dr. Fred Carter
5219 Deer creek Rd., WICHITA FALLS,
TX 76302, USA
Phone: (940) 723-4020
email: fcarter@wf.quik.com

Edmund Davidson
3345 Virginia Avenue, Goshen,
VA 24439, USA
Phone: (540) 997 5651
Site: http://www.edmunddavidson.com/
ed_mainframe.htm

Jose de Braga
229, de la Martiniere, Quebec,
PQ, Canada G1L 4G7
Phone: (418) 948 0105
email: josecdebraga@globetrotter.net
Site: http://www.geocities.com/
josedebraga/aboutme.html

Jim Ence
145 S 200 E.
Richfield, Utah 84701 USA
Phone: (435) 896-6206

Jerry Fisk
10095 Highway 278 West
Nashville, AR 71852, USA
Phone: (870) 845-4456
email: jerry@fisk-knives.com
Site: http://www.fisk-knives.com

Larry Fuegen
617 N. Coulter Circle
Prescott, AZ 86303-6270, USA
Phone/Fax: (928) 776-8777
email: fuegen@cableone.net

Chantal Gilbert
291 rue Christophe Colomb est, #105
Ville de Québec, Canada, G1K-3T1
Phone: (418) 525-6961
Fax: (418) 525-4666
email: gilbertc@mediom.qc.ca
Site: http://www.chantalgilbert.com

Tim Hancock
10805 N 83rd Street, Scottsdale,
AZ 85260, USA
Phone: (480) 998-8849
email: timhancock@aol.com

Gil Hibben
2914 Winters Lane (P.O.Box 13),
LaGrange KY 40031, USA
Phone (shop): (502) 222-1397
Phone (home): (502) 222-4090
Fax: (502) 222-2676
email: gil_hibben@ earthlink.net
Site: http://www.hibbenknives.com

D'Alton Holder
7148, W. Country Gables Dr.,
Peoria, AZ 85381, USA
Phone: (623) 878-3064
Fax: (623) 878-3964
email: dholderknives@cox.net
Site: http://www.dholder.com

Paul M. Jarvis
30 Chalk Street, Cambridge,
MA 02139, USA
Phone: home (617) 547-4355
work: (617) 666-9090

John L. Jensen
530 S, Madison #14
PASADENA, CA 91101, USA
Phone: (626) 449-1148
email: john@jensenknives.com
Site: http://www.jensenknives.com

Gay Rocha, USA

Making knives since 1974, Gay Rocha
lives in the mountains of Oregon as an
impoverished artisan.

"The Mayor's Mistress"

Commissioned in 1997, the 20" (508 mm)
fantasy knife took 6 months to complete.
It is made of carbon steel, forge-welded
and then ground to shape.

The inserts are fossil mammoth ivory and
the sheath is forged of mild steel, lined
with ABS plastic and has a corian throat.
The knife locks automatically in its sheath
and is mechanically released by pressing
a thumb lever. For collectors to safely
fondle his intentioned sensuality, Gay
prefers to deliver his knives unsharpened.

Featured Artists (cont.)

S. R. Johnson
202 E. 200 N. (P. O. Box 5)
Manti, UT 84642, USA
Phone/Fax: (435) 835-7941
email: srj@manti.com
Site: http://www.srjknives.com

Dietmar Kressler
Schloss Odelzhausen,
Schlossberg 1 - 85235 Odelzhausen,
Germany
Phone: (+49) 8134 7759
(+49) 8135 993967
Fax: (+49) 8134 559576

Francesco Pachi
Via Pometta, 1
17046 SASSELLO (SV), Italy
Tel/Fax: (+39) 019 720086
email: info@pachi-knives.com
Site: http://www.pachi-knives.com

Conny Persson
Ryggskog 588
S-820 50 LOS, SWEDEN
Phone (workshop): (+46) 657 10305
Cellphone: (+46) 703213355
email: connyknives@swipnet.se
Site: http://www.connyknives.com

Pierre Reverdy
5 Rue De L'egallite
26100 Romans, FRANCE
Phone: (+33) 4 7505 1015
FAX: (+33) 4 7502 2840
email: reverdy-piel@wanadoo.fr
Site: http://www.reverdy.com

Scott Slobodian
4101, River Ridge Drive, (P.O.Box 1498)
San Andreas, CA 95249, USA
Phone: (209) 286-1980
Fax: (209) 286-1982
email: scott@slobodianswords.com
Site: http://www.slobodianswords.com

Dwight L. Towell
2375 Towell Rd.
Midvale, ID 83645, USA
Phone: (208) 355-2419

Buster Warenski
590 E 500 N,
Richfield, UT 84701, USA
Phone: (435) 896-5319
email: buster@warenskiknives.com
Site: www.warenskiknives.com

Yoshindo Yoshihara
8-17-11 Takasago, Katsushika-Ku,
Tokyo 125, JAPAN
Phone: (+81) 33607 5255
Fax: (+81) 33607 1405
In the USA: c/o Leon Kapp (Lonnie)
49 Point San Pedro Rd., San Rafael,
CA 94901, USA
Phone: (415) 457-6436
Fax: (415) 459-4791
email: leonkapp@aol.com

Owen Wood, USA

Born 1951 in South Africa, Owen began my knife-making career in the seventies, his early work being primarily functional. His wife, Sue, who is an artist, initiated his thirst to combine form and function and so began the journey of discovery into the fascinating world of applied art, Art Noveau and Art Deco, perhaps being the movements, that have had most influence upon his own style.

"Crown of Thorns" Dagger, 2003

This is a collaborative work. Daniel Kronberg, miniature sculptor, created the bronze rosebud forming the pommel of the dagger and the marvelous bronze guard of thorny rose vines from which the the blade emerges. Owen continued the rose vine theme into the blade in the form of wavy nickel lines captured by the outer blade panels of fine left and right twist Damascus and forged into a single composite blade. The haft is ancient walrus ivory.

Overall length 11 1/2"(293 mm).

One page displays and others

André Andersson
Forsnäsvägen 40 918 92 Bullmark, Sweden
Phone: (+46) 90 56216
email: northland@swipnet.se
Site: http://www.northland.nu

Ron Appleton
P.O. Box 118 Bluff Dale, TX. 76433, U.S.A
Phone: (254) 728-3039
email: ron@helovesher.com

Todd Begg
420 169th Street, South
Spanaway, WA 98387, USA
Phone: (253) 531-2113
email: tntbegg@comcast.net
Site: www.beggknives.com

Vladimir Burkovski
P.O.Box 4591 Haifa 31044, Israel
Phone: (+972) 54-499-3902
email: burkovskiart@yahoo.com
Site: www.knifearts.com

Dave Cowles
214 Quarry Road
Spartanburg, SC 29302, USA
email: Dave@DaveCowles.net
Site: www.CowlesDesign.com

Don Cowles
1026 Lawndale Dr.
Royal Oak, MI 48067, USA
Phone: (248) 541-4619
email: don@cowlesknives.com
Site: http://www.cowlesknives.com

Dellana
168 Riverbend Blvd.,
St. Albans, WV 25177, USA
Phone: (304) 727-5512
email: DELLANA@charter.net
Site: http://www.dellana.cc

Lloyd Hale
3492 Ker Hill Road
Lynnville, Tenn 38472, USA
Phone: (931) 424-5846
email: lloydhale@surfmore.net

Billy Mace Imel
1616 Bundy Ave., New Castle
IN 47362, USA, Phone: (765) 529-1651

Leon Kapp (Lonnie)
49 Point San Pedro Rd., San Rafael,
CA 94901, USA
Phone: (415) 457-6436
Fax: (415) 459-4791
email: leonkapp@aol.com

Linda Karst Stone
402 Hwy. 27 East, Ingram
Texas 78025-3317, USA
Phone/Fax: (830) 896-4678
email: karstone@ktc.com

Jim Kelso
577 Collar Hill Road
Worcester, VT 05682, USA
Phone: (802) 229-4254
email: tooluser@sover.net
Site: http://www.arscives.com/jkelso

Wolfgang Loerchner
13 Glass Street,
Bayfield, Ontario, CANADA N0M 1G0
email: loerchner@tcc.on.ca
Phone: (519) 565-2196

Bob Loveless
4333 Tyler Street, Riverside, CA 92503, USA
Phone: (909) 689-7800

Larry C. Mensch
578 Madison Avenue
Milton, PA 17847, USA
Phone: (570) 742-9554

William F. Moran
6612 Jefferson Blvd., Braddock Hights,
MD 21714, USA
Phone: (301) 371-7543

Dusty Moulton
135 Hillview Lane Loudon, TN 37774, USA
Phone: 865-408-9779
email: dusty@moultonknives.com
Site: http://www.moultonknives.com

Ron Newton
223 Ridge Lane, London, AR 72847, USA
Phone: (479) 293-3001

Zaza Revishvili
2102 Linden Ave. Madison, WI 53704, USA
Phone/Fax: (608) 243-7927
email: zazaint1@aol.com

Gay Rocha
183 Rock View Lane
GLIDE, Oregon 97443, USA
Phone: (541) 496-4100

Jan Slezak
Mendlova 1535, Nove Mesto na Morave,
592 31, Czech Republic.
Phone (Home): 566 616 868
Phone (Mobile): 737 344 925

Gary Williams (Garbo)
email: williamg@infionline.net

Owen D. Wood
6492 Garrison St., Arvada, CO 80004, USA
Phone: 303-456-2748
Fax: 303-456-2748
email: owen.wood@att.net
Site: http://www.owenwoodcustomknives.com

Dr. David Darom
1 Haim Bajayo St., Jerusalem 93145, Israel
Phone: (+972) 2-5665885
email: ddd@cc.huji.ac.il
Site: http://www.david-darom.com

Paolo Saviolo (Italy)
Tipografia Edizioni Saviolo
Via Col di Lana, 12-13100 Vercelli, ITALY
Phone: (+39) 0161-391000
Fax: (+39) 0161-271256
email: paolo@tipografiaedizionisaviolo.191.it
psaviolo@tin.it

Paolo Saviolo (USA)
Saviolo Publishing House
P O Box 2675
Mandeville, Louisiana 70470-2675, USA
Phone: (985) 792-0115 Fax: (985) 792-0199
email: ssj@saviolopublisher.com

Larry Mensch, USA

Born in 1937, Larry has been a full time knifemaker since
1993. He lives in Milton, Pennsylvania with his wife
Connie. Best known for high-end, fancy "users", this
highly energetic, prolific knifemaker creates fixed blades
of all types and sizes, every now and then letting his
considerable imagination soar with flights of fancy such
as the dagger featured here.

The **"Dragonfly" dagger (2004)** was a dream brought
to life by Larry Mensch. Fashioned from Damasteel in the
form of a dragonfly, the handle is made of ebony with
ivory spacers, embellished with silver chain, and topped
off with a 10mm industrial ruby.

Overall legth 8 1/4" (210 mm).

Related Books

Allara Roberto and Silvano G. Mapelli, ***Hand-Crafted Knives***, Priuli & Verlucca, 1999.

Darom David, Dr., ***Art and Design in Modern Custom Folding Knives***, DDD and Tipografia Edizioni Saviolo, 2003.

Hughes B. R. and C. Houston Price, ***Master of the Forge***, Knife World Books, 1996.

Kapp Leon and Hiroko and Yoshindo Yoshihara, ***The Craft of the Japanese Sword***, Kodansha International, 1987.

Kapp Leon and Hiroko and Yoshindo Yoshihara, ***Modern Japanese Swords and Swordsmiths***, Kodansha International, 2002.

Kertzman Joe, 24th Annual ***KNIVES 2004***, Krause Publications, 2003.

Kertzman Joe, 25th Annual ***KNIVES 2005***, Krause Publications, 2004.

Levine Bernard, ***Knifemakers of Old San Francisco***, BADGER Books, 1977.

Zaza Revishvili, USA

Born in 1962, the "good old days of the USSR", in Tbilisi the capital of the Georgian Republic, Zaza resides now in the USA. He acquired his deep knowledge of the arts at the Tbilisi State Academy of Arts in 1985 and his main goal is to create true art form using unique craftsmanship techniques.

"Farrow Ramzres", 2001

Considered by Zaza as one of his finest designs, he used Jerry Fisk's Turkish pattern Damascus for the blade. The sheath and handle are covered in silver filigree, an ancient technique of soldering hand twisted silver wires with silver solder. The stones are AA grade natural garnets. Overall length 14 1/2" (292 mm).

This Bob Loveless knife, made in the early 80s, was sent to the author as a gift by Dr. Thad Kawakami-Wong of Hawaii, a friend and an enthusiastic knife collector. Thad explained in a note he later sent by email: *"David, good you have received the Loveless and I am happy you like it. I needed to thank you for such a marvelous book that you did (Custom Folding Knives). I also wanted to express my deepest thanks for providing others who will never attend a knife show an opportunity to see what knife collecting is all about. Now it is possible for others to see and maybe understand why we spend so much time, money and effort into buying art knives. Ok my friend, most people talk, I like to show with actions so I told myself that I should send you this knife as a gift. Aloha, Thad".*